ALLEN V. KNEESE
CHARLES L. SCHULTZE

Pollution, Prices, and Public Policy

BROOKINGS

POLLUTION, PRICES,
AND PUBLIC POLICY

ALLEN V. KNEESE
CHARLES L. SCHULTZE

POLLUTION, PRICES, AND PUBLIC POLICY

A study sponsored jointly by
RESOURCES FOR THE FUTURE, INC.
and
THE BROOKINGS INSTITUTION

THE BROOKINGS INSTITUTION
Washington, D.C.

Library of Congress Cataloging in Publication Data:

Kneese, Allen V
   Pollution, prices, and public policy.
   1. Environmental policy—United States.
2. Environmental policy—United States—Finance.
3. Environmental law—United States. I. Schultze,
Charles L., joint author. II. Title.
HC110.E5K57   301.31′0973   74-1432
ISBN 0-8157-4994-5
ISBN 0-8157-4993-7 pbk.

9 8 7 6 5 4 3 2

THE BROOKINGS INSTITUTION is an independent organization devoted to nonpartisan research, education, and publication in economics, government, foreign policy, and the social sciences generally. Its principal purposes are to aid in the development of sound public policies and to promote public understanding of issues of national importance.

The Institution was founded on December 8, 1927, to merge the activities of the Institute for Government Research, founded in 1916, the Institute of Economics, founded in 1922, and the Robert Brookings Graduate School of Economics and Government, founded in 1924.

The Board of Trustees is responsible for the general administration of the Institution, while the immediate direction of the policies, program, and staff is vested in the President, assisted by an advisory committee of the officers and staff. The by-laws of the Institution state, "It is the function of the Trustees to make possible the conduct of scientific research, and publication, under the most favorable conditions, and to safeguard the independence of the research staff in the pursuit of their studies and in the publication of the results of such studies. It is not a part of their function to determine, control, or influence the conduct of particular investigations or the conclusions reached."

The President bears final responsibility for the decision to publish a manuscript as a Brookings book or staff paper. In reaching his judgment on the competence, accuracy, and objectivity of each study, the President is advised by the director of the appropriate research program and weighs the views of a panel of expert outside readers who report to him in confidence on the quality of the work. Publication of a work signifies that it is deemed to be a competent treatment worthy of public consideration; such publication does not imply endorsement of conclusions or recommendations contained in the study.

The Institution maintains its position of neutrality on issues of public policy in order to safeguard the intellectual freedom of the staff. Hence interpretations or conclusions in Brookings publications should be understood to be solely those of the author or authors and should not be attributed to the Institution, to its trustees, officers, or other staff members, or to the organizations that support its research.

Foreword

RISING national concern over domestic supplies of energy throws into sharp relief the difficult problems that confront Americans in seeking a cleaner environment. If electric utilities burn coal instead of oil, we reduce dependence on imports but we risk befouling the air. If we stripmine low-sulfur western coal or exploit oil shale, we may help keep the air free of sulfur but we may also despoil hundreds of square miles of western land and pollute the tributaries of western rivers.

The nation has decided in favor of a cleaner environment. But it is equally committed to economic growth and a rising standard of living. The problem is that these goals, to some extent, conflict with each other.

Conflict among important goals cannot be eliminated, but the authors' theme in this book is that pollution control programs can be designed to reduce substantially the costs of cleaning up the environment, and to cope more flexibly with the difficult choices the energy outlook imposes. After outlining the major economic and technical aspects of air and water pollution, the authors examine the basic legislation under which U.S. pollution control programs now operate. That legislation, they conclude, has led to increasingly detailed federal regulation of business firms and industries and has fostered generous subsidies to firms and municipalities for the construction of waste treatment facilities. They spell out the enforcement difficulties, the high enforcement costs, and the loss of flexibility that these approaches entail, and argue that interactions between the environment and the economy are far too complex and subtle to be mastered by a regulatory bureaucracy.

They then present an alternative strategy with two central components: a set of national effluent and emission charges—taxes levied on each unit of air- and water-polluting substance discharged

by a firm or municipality into the environment—and the creation
of a set of regional authorities, under federal guidelines, to undertake the large-scale planning and public works construction needed
for effective control of pollution in entire river basins or in the air
above whole regions. Arguing that the imposition of "pollution
taxes" would channel the incentives and creativity of the industrial
system toward a cleaner environment by the powerful device of
making the reduction of pollution a paying proposition, they cite
empirical studies to support their conclusion that this approach
would substantially reduce the cost and improve the effectiveness of
air and water pollution control programs.

Allen V. Kneese, a member of the economics faculty at the
University of New Mexico, was in charge of research on the quality
of the environment at Resources for the Future until May 1974. He
is the author of or a contributor to many books and articles on the
economics of environmental quality. Charles L. Schultze, a Brookings senior fellow and a member of the economics faculty at the
University of Maryland, is the author or co-author of several Brookings books and a former director of the U.S. Bureau of the Budget.

This book arose from a joint project of the Brookings Institution
and Resources for the Future, Inc., that was supported by grants
from the Carnegie Corporation and the Richard King Mellon
Foundation. The authors benefited greatly from the comments of
many people on earlier drafts of the manuscript, and especially
wish to thank Blair P. Bower, Nina Cornell, J. Clarence Davies,
Edwin T. Haefele, Jack L. Knetsch, and Alice M. Rivlin. Frederick
C. Ribe provided research assistance. Evelyn P. Fisher checked the
book for factual errors. Brenda L. Dixon and Vera A. Ullrich provided secretarial assistance. Mendelle T. Berenson edited the manuscript; Florence Robinson prepared the index.

The views expressed here are those of the authors and should not
be ascribed to any of the persons whose assistance is acknowledged
above or to the trustees, officers, or other staff members of the
Brookings Institution, or to Resources for the Future, the Carnegie
Corporation, or the Richard King Mellon Foundation.

KERMIT GORDON *President*
The Brookings Institution

November 1974
Washington, D.C.

MARION CLAWSON *Acting President*
Resources for the Future, Inc.

Contents

Tables

Figures

CHAPTER ONE

The Issues

OVER THE PAST two decades a body of federal policy has gradually developed to deal with air and water pollution on a national basis. That policy has had two central components: first, increasingly detailed federal regulations, limiting the amount of pollutants that business firms, municipalities, and consumers may discharge into the environment; and second, increasingly large subsidies to municipalities and business firms for the construction of plants to treat waste water.

The development of federal policy culminated in two comprehensive pieces of legislation—the Clean Air Amendments of 1970 and the Federal Water Pollution Control Act Amendments of 1972. These acts substantially enlarged and strengthened the regulatory and subsidy elements of federal policy, and committed the nation to an ambitious set of goals for clean air and water. Despite the easing of some of the requirements regarding air pollution control in the face of the energy crisis of 1973–74, and the apparent displacement of concern about pollution by concern over fuel supplies, efforts at environmental control will continue to have a major impact on the nation. If carried out as intended, current pollution control laws will require over the next decade expenditures of up to half a trillion dollars by consumers, business firms, and governments, and substantial changes in industrial practices and the style of consumer living.

This study seeks to evaluate the pollution control strategy that has emerged over the past two decades, and to contrast that strategy with an alternative approach. We conclude that the current strategy, with its reliance on detailed regulation and construction subsidies, is likely to be excessively costly and dependent for its effectiveness on an omniscience that a regulatory bureaucracy cannot be expected to possess. The alternative we suggest places greater reliance

1

on techniques that modify the incentives facing private decision makers so that in hard dollars and cents it pays them to reduce pollution and costs them dearly not to. This change of incentives would be accomplished by levying a stiff tax on every unit of pollution discharged into the air or water. In addition we stress the creation of region-wide agencies for air and water pollution control, which can plan and develop integrated measures not achievable through regulation or construction subsidies for individual waste treatment plants. We believe that evidence from studies of pollution control problems demonstrates that the incentive-oriented alternative, while no panacea, would be more effective and far less costly than the current national strategy for controlling pollution.

The Emergence of Pollution Control as a National Issue

On November 16, 1960, the President's Commission on National Goals, composed of eleven distinguished citizens, delivered to President Dwight D. Eisenhower its report, *Goals for Americans*. The report listed fifteen major goals, each of which the commission felt to be an area for national concern and action in the coming decade, but controlling environmental pollution was not on the list. The report was accompanied by fifteen major papers, one on each of the subject areas, prepared by recognized experts. In the 372 pages of the volume, five short paragraphs were devoted to the problem of air and water pollution. This minimal attention to the environment probably reflected accurately the nation's consciousness of the subject at the beginning of the last decade.[1]

In a short five years, by the mid-1960s, environmental control had moved toward the top of the list of nationally perceived problems. While energy problems suddenly came to the fore in 1973, concern with pollution is not a passing fad. Environmental problems are real; dealing with them will get harder as the years go by. Americans have come to understand that clean air and water are

1. This is not to say that no professional or public attention was paid to pollution problems much earlier. Waterborne disease, a major problem in the first decades of this century, was successfully dealt with through the development of effective treatment processes for drinking water. In another celebrated case, smoke control came to Pittsburgh after pollution became a strong local issue. Also, as later chapters report, some weak federal legislation was put on the books in the forties and fifties. Not until the sixties, however, did pollution control arouse wide popular concern.

not inexhaustible in supply, but sharply limited. And a modern industrial society assaults the air and water with tremendous volumes of poisonous wastes. As economic growth and urbanization proceed, unchecked discharges of pollutants would turn America's inland and coastal waterways into noxious sewers, and blanket its cities with smog far worse than they already experience. And while less is known about their effects, heat, carbon dioxide, and other by-products of civilization could conceivably damage the global environment seriously. Yet we do not want to give up the advances in living standards that economic growth provides. And the overwhelming weight of evidence to date is that, with careful management, we can have our cake and eat it too—we can reconcile economic growth with a reasonably clean environment. The application of modern technology made it possible in the United States to halve the amount of labor per unit of production every twenty-five to thirty years. The same ingenuity could enable us similarly to reduce, sharply and steadily, the harmful environmental by-products of modern civilization. The technical means are available to deal with the problem or can be found, but doing so will require a major national effort under a workable national policy.

Controlling environmental damage raises far more than technological problems, however. The impact of industry, agriculture, and urban society on the environment is both pervasive and complex. There are perhaps 55,000 major industrial sources of water pollution in the United States, in different industries, with different processes, facing different economic conditions, and located on watercourses with different environmental characteristics. Most of the nation's meat and poultry production is now concentrated in large feedlots whose wastes frequently run off unchecked into rivers and streams—and one head of beef is equivalent to sixteen humans in potential water pollution. About 120 million automobiles, trucks, and buses spew forth pollutants. Controlling one form of pollution often generates others: municipal waste treatment plants must dispose of a growing volume of sludge; replacement of coal by nuclear fuel for utility plants reduces sulfur emissions but increases waste heat and generates radioactive wastes. Oil is generally cleaner to burn than coal, but has suddenly become hard to get and very expensive. Moreover, almost every situation offers a number of ways to reduce pollution that differ widely in effectiveness and cost. Be-

4 Pollution, Prices, and Public Policy

cause environmental effects permeate every aspect of economic life, control of those effects must be equally pervasive.

Environmental Pollution and the Failure of Incentives

Insight into the nature and scale of modern environmental pollution was slow to develop in the economics profession, as it was in most other pertinent disciplines. Recently, however, the joint application of two basic concepts—*conservation of mass* and *common-property resources*—has significantly improved our understanding of the environmental problem.

The law of conservation of mass is one of the most elementary concepts of physics: matter is created or destroyed only in the most minute amounts. Man uses the materials of nature in various ways —he eats and drinks them, heats them, burns them, extracts metals and chemical compounds from them, and combines them into manufactured goods—but he does not physically destroy them. He consumes the services or utilities that physical objects yield, but not the objects themselves. Materials come from nature, are used, and are returned (usually in different form) to the earth, the air, or the water, as "residuals" with no loss in their mass.[2] The return of residuals to nature can damage the environment, either because in the process of using original materials man has transformed them into something harmful (toxic chemicals, for example) and has concentrated them in unnatural ways (sewage from a city or a feedlot), or because otherwise harmless residuals react chemically with other substances or with each other in the air or water in a damaging way (as in the reaction of hydrocarbons from auto emissions with sunlight and oxides of nitrogen to form smog).

Common-property resources are those that for a variety of reasons are not held in private ownership but are in some vague sense collectively held—not really under any one person's or institution's managerial control. Among the most important of these resources are water bodies, the air mantle, and various other ecological systems.

In an earlier day a smaller and more dispersed population and a

2. In subatomic reactions, mass can be converted into energy. But the vast bulk of man's use of materials involves chemical and biological actions in which mass is never destroyed.

much lower level of economic activity did not generally tax the capacity of air and water to assimilate wastes. These common-property resources were in such abundance that they came close to furnishing perfect examples of the economist's category of free goods. But as population, urbanization, and economic activity grew, what were once plentiful environmental resources became increasingly scarce. Nevertheless, the nation continued to treat them as if they were free goods. Smog-laden air and unsightly, foul-smelling, and unhealthy rivers are manifestations of the failure of U.S. institutions to cope successfully with the deepening scarcity of air and water and the need somehow to ration them to their best uses.

In most circumstances the price system provides incentives for economizing on scarce resources. Those who use such resources must pay for them, at a price that reflects the scarcity. Goods whose production requires scarce resources in large amounts are expensive compared with those that do not, so consumption of the former is discouraged and use of the latter is encouraged. Business firms, motivated by the search for profits—indeed, by the need to survive—seek ways to minimize the use of costly resources in their production processes. But since the waste-assimilating capacities of air and water as common-property resources do not command a price, the private market system encourages their overuse rather than their conservation. The production of bleached household paper products generates ten times the level of some water pollutants that unbleached paper does. But since the paper mill does not pay for pollution damage, the prices of bleached paper products do not reflect their true costs, and consumers have no incentive to use the unbleached product. At some expense, food processors can modify their canning processes to reduce sharply the amount of wastes poured into the water. But since they are not charged for the damages that their wastes create, why undertake the added expense?

The problem is not that the price system does not work—it works with marvelous efficiency, but in the wrong direction. When the signals it sends out indicate that air and water are free goods, thousands of firms and millions of consumers bend their efforts to use those cheap resources. And so electric utilities dispose of the sulfur residuals from coal and oil not by scrubbing them from their stacks or by other expensive means, but by pouring them freely into the atmosphere. Paper mills use the rivers as free dumps for noxious chemicals. And consumers avoid the cost of eliminating hydrocarbon emissions from their automobiles by depositing them in the air.

The free use of the air and water as dumps for residuals, therefore, creates a situation in which the costs and prices of goods and services diverge in varying degrees from the true costs that their production and consumption impose on society. The greater the environmental damage caused by the residuals from any particular production or consumption activity, the greater the divergence. The price system conveys the false message that society places no value on clean air and water. The economy reacts accordingly.

Even with a proper set of incentives and signals, however, some aspects of pollution control are beyond the actions of individual producers or consumers. In some circumstances, for example, water pollution can be reduced most efficiently by large-scale public works—dams that store water in periods of high flow for release during periods of low flow to reduce the concentration of pollution, or aeration devices that pump oxygen into the water to restore its life-giving qualities for wildlife. Some form of regional water quality authorities is needed to plan, finance, and execute control measures along entire river basins. Similarly, regional land-use planning, possibly implemented by effective incentive schemes and control over the way public works are provided, can have an important effect on air and water pollution discharges and on the degree of harm they do.

Clearly, the massive return of residuals to the common-property environmental resources confronts us with a severe problem. The problem arises primarily because the institutions of private property and exchange that we use for determining the value of resources and providing incentives for their efficient allocation cannot function for environmental resources. We thus face a large-scale, pervasive, and unfamiliar problem of collective action and collective management.

The Broader Problem of Incentives

While this paper deals with public policy toward control of air and water pollution, the shortcomings of that policy are common to a much wider class of cases. For a variety of reasons, mainly though not solely stemming from the increasing interdependence of the various parts of modern society, the federal government is called upon to intervene in the production and distribution of particular goods and services. Private decisions about automobiles and mass transit result in urban congestion and smog. Individual actions of private physicians, hospitals, and insurance companies cumulate, pushing up medical costs and leaving some parts of the nation without adequate health care. Poor patterns of utilization create surpluses of railroad freight cars in some areas while others have none in which to ship their products to market. The vagaries of private development spawn suburban sprawl and inner-city decay. Increasing private investment on the flood plains along major rivers aggravates the damage from the large floods that nature sporadically decrees. In each of these cases something is amiss in a very complicated system of economic and social relationships. Confronting the need to do something about the situation, the American political system tends to generate laws and administrative arrangements that share several characteristics.

First, public policy dealing with such problems relies heavily on a regulatory approach. Administrative bodies are charged with drawing up rules of detailed behavior that specify what is allowable and what is not. Accordingly, little effort is put into devising new incentives or correcting existing ones to spur individual decision makers, in their own self-interest, toward socially desirable actions. To control medical costs under Medicare and Medicaid, a huge volume of regulations for hospitals and other health care institutions has been written. Yet the federal government pays hospitals for medical services under "cost-plus" arrangements that virtually invite rapid escalation of costs. The unavailability of freight cars stems not from an overall shortage of freight cars but from inefficient use of those already in existence. Under the current system of charges, a railroad has no incentive to make efficient use of the cars owned by another railroad. Rather than devise a system of incentive charges, the Interstate Commerce Commission issues specific orders to railroads to return empty cars to shortage areas. So far the approach to pollution control has developed in the same pattern—central regulation of the actions of individual polluters.

The regulatory approach has not been notable for its effectiveness. Regulatory agencies have often become the captives of the industries they are charged with overseeing. Much of the regulatory effort in the field of transportation seems to have been aimed at insulating the various forms of transportation from competition with each other. In the case of Medicare and Medicaid, regulations continually expand in number and complexity as the regulated providers of health care find new ways of getting around old regulations. Almost inevitably, the interactions and nuances of complicated social systems begin to overwhelm the regulators. One set of regulations creates unintended problems, which then call forth yet a new set. All of these problems will be intensified in the case of pollution control regulations, because of the pervasiveness and complexity of environmental problems.

Second, legislative approaches to many problems arising in the private sector of the economy tend to rely heavily on subsidies for the construction of capital facilities. While occasionally appropriate, construction subsidies are usually inefficient in dealing with social problems. Federal flood control projects often seek to protect investments that should never have been made in the flood plains in the first place. And because only nominal charges are levied on the beneficiaries, additional investments in high-risk areas are encouraged, so that flood damages continue to mount. To meet the problem of auto congestion, the capital costs of mass transit systems are subsidized. And so, expensive capital-intensive subway systems are arbitrarily favored over more flexible bus systems; and purchases of new equipment are stimulated while repair, maintenance, and improvements in service are ignored. The shortage of medical care in inner cities and rural areas is addressed by subsidies for building hospitals rather than subsidies for providing health care, as a result of which far too much medical care is delivered in the most expensive way possible. Urban wastes dumped into the nation's streams are handled by federal subsidies for constructing large waste treatment works, too often built in the wrong places—and then run inefficiently. A public subsidy may often be necessary to deal with failures of the private economic system. But wherever possible, the political system concentrates those subsidies on monumental construction projects, often ignoring the need for more fundamental changes. As a consequence, unnecessarily expensive solutions are promoted, since construction is subsidized to the neglect of other techniques for dealing with the situation. Problems that arise from basic failures of incentives in the private economy cannot be smothered in concrete and steel—although ribbon-cutting and dedication ceremonies do generate good publicity for the officials responsible.

The Problem of Complexity

The design of public programs in the United States, especially outside the field of defense policy, is usually decided through an adversary process. On most policy issues there is a wide range of conflicting views reflecting the diversity of interests in a continental nation of 210 million people. The legislative process in the Congress is a marvelous device for negotiation, compromise, and ultimate reconciliation of views, so that on important decisions a large majority of the nation will be in agreement, or at worst not hostile to the ultimate outcome. The hearings, interest-group lobbying, back-room horsetrading, floor amendments, and conferences that characterize the way in which legislation is designed, are well suited to this purpose. Conflicting opinions on *what* goals public policy ought to set for itself are harmonized at the national level by these institutions of the Congress. As society becomes more complex and public goals more ambitious, however, technical problems of *how* government best goes about achieving its ends take on more importance. Deciding the magnitude of social security benefits or veterans' pensions or investment in national parks requires the reconciliation of divergent views, but imposes no major problems about the means of achieving the goals finally agreed upon. However, when the federal government sets about dealing with situations that are inherently complex, and that involve literally millions of interactions among individuals, state and local governments, and business firms, then *how* becomes as critical as *what*. Furthermore, since *how* can greatly influence costs, it becomes intermingled with the question of *what*.

Pollution control is a case in point. As we have already pointed out, and as the next chapter discusses in some detail, each year literally millions of business and consumer decisions have environmental impacts. In turn, pollution control decisions have major effects on industrial location, economic costs, and living standards. Moreover, the technical relationships between economic decisions and the environment are highly complicated. The obvious remedies sometimes turn out to have unwanted side-effects; for example, re-moving pollutants from water may create troublesome problems of sludge disposal. Environmental problems are by no means the only ones that raise knotty technical issues in the design of public pro-grams, but they are a good illustration of the general case.

When the problem is one of reconciling sharply differing views about the objectives of public policy, the staff, the information, and the criteria for evaluating alternative proposals upon which the Congress now relies serve its needs well. But when the success of public policy depends upon systematic consideration of strategically different policy approaches and the design of sophisticated tech-niques to deal with complicated situations, different kinds of per-sonnel, information, and evaluation criteria are needed—and these are not now generally available to the Congress. An analysis of this lack as it has affected the development of pollution control policy will, we hope, shed some light on the more general question of how the legislative process can deal more effectively with broad policy alternatives and complicated technical issues.

Plan of the Study

The next chapter summarizes the major economic and technical facts about air and water pollution, as a necessary background for understanding the problems that beset control policy. The sub-sequent four chapters discuss existing national policies toward air and water pollution control—their legislative history, enforcement problems, and economic costs. In chapter 7 alternative control strategies are outlined and compared with current policy in terms of effectiveness and cost. A short epilogue returns to the broader question touched on above: Why does the political system behave as it does with respect to these problems? Drawing on the history of pollution control legislation, we suggest some reasons why public intervention in complex matters of economic policy tends to be biased toward the regulatory and the construction-subsidy tech-niques, and pays too little attention to other alternatives. We con-clude by offering several suggestions for improved legislative han-dling of complicated policy issues.

CHAPTER TWO

Some Technical Background

CONTROLLING POLLUTION is, both technically and politically, an exceedingly difficult problem for public policy. We can start with four central facts.

1. *The assimilative capacities of air and water are valuable assets to a society.* Yet, long after these qualities became scarce and valuable, societies—including our own—continued to treat them as if they were limitless, allowing individuals, municipalities, and industries to use them freely. Because they carried no price, no one felt any need to economize on their use. Pollution arises, therefore, because the institutional arrangements of society have positively encouraged heavy use of environmental assets.

2. *The nation now wants cleaner air and cleaner water and looks to the federal government as the principal agent to secure them.* Whatever the disagreement about how ambitious the objectives of environmental control policy should be, a wide consensus holds that pollution must be reduced below its present level and that future growth in production and population should not be allowed to undo the initial efforts.

3. *Reducing pollution is expensive.* The cost of constructing and operating municipal waste treatment plants adds to the tax bill. Reducing industrial pollution of air and water adds to the cost of production, sometimes slows down the exploitation of domestic energy sources, and ultimately increases prices paid by consumers. Moreover, the costs of pollution control rise very steeply as the targets for environmental cleanliness become more ambitious.

4. *Both air and water pollution are exceedingly complex phenomena.* Policy making must wrestle with the technical difficulty of tracing pollution in the air or water to specific sources. It must take account of the fact that in almost every industry and every

11

situation there are alternative ways to reduce pollution that vary widely in effectiveness and cost. It must recognize that reducing one kind of pollution sometimes increases another, and that the greater the success of controlling one type, the more likely are these "spill-over" effects. And finally it must operate in a world of imperfect knowledge, in which the relative cost and effectiveness of various abatement devices, and the interaction of pollutants with the environment, are subject to great uncertainty.

Given these facts, federal policies designed to deal with pollution should meet three essential criteria. In face of a very complex situation, control policy should be *effective and enforceable* so as to achieve expeditiously the reduction in pollution that the nation clearly wants. It must be *flexible* so that we are not locked into uniform technological choices before we have good information on their costs and consequences. And since the costs of pollution control are inevitably large and will ultimately be borne by consumers and taxpayers, poor as well as rich, control policy should be *efficient*—that is, it should seek the least-cost means of achieving whatever environmental standards the nation decides on.

In order to evaluate alternative public policies in the light of these three criteria, some understanding of the basic facts about environmental pollution is indispensable. This chapter seeks to provide the bare minimum background in three areas: (1) the nature of the interactions between economic activities and the environment, and the kinds of damage those interactions bring about; (2) the variety of means available to reduce or eliminate damage; and (3) some economic aspects of environmental pollution and its control.

The Kinds of Environmental Damage

Can man's activities be on such a vast scale as to upset the global balance of nature? The burning of fossil fuels adds carbon dioxide and particulates to the atmosphere. Carbon dioxide absorbs the sun's infrared radiation, and a large enough increase in its concentration in the atmosphere could raise the temperature of the Earth, with potentially damaging consequences including melting of parts of the polar icecaps and a rise in the level of the oceans. Particulate matter affects the Earth's climate by scattering and absorbing sunlight and by causing water vapor to condense and form clouds with definite, if as yet unmeasured, net effects. Man's generation of energy also pours heat directly into the atmosphere in amounts large enough to alter the climate in local areas.

Global effects like these are extremely difficult to measure and forecast. And some of them work in offsetting directions. There is much controversy over what directions they might take and just how serious they might become if economic growth throughout the world continues at its present pace for another century. Broader understanding of these kinds of interactions and a start on monitoring them much more systematically are plainly in order. Also, the development of analytical models to help in understanding and forecasting them is an urgent matter. Should it become necessary to cut back sharply on the rate at which mankind converts fuels to energy, massive economic and political adjustments will be called for.

But these are not the problems that this study addresses. The concern here is with the clear and present regional and local problems of air and water pollution, whose effects, while not so potentially cataclysmic as those discussed above, already inflict major damages on society, and so far have been the main concerns of environmental policy at the federal level in the United States.

Water Pollution

One way of looking at the damaging residuals discharged into the watercourses is to begin by dividing them into three major categories. These are the *degradable,* the *nondegradable,* and the *persistent* pollutants.

Degradable wastes are organic residuals, upon which bacteria and other micro-organisms can feed; bacteria themselves; and energy (heat) which is gradually dissipated from the watercourse to the air. Domestic sewage is the most commonly known organic waste, but industrial wastes from the chemical, food processing, pulp and paper, petroleum refining, and other industries, together with the runoff from agricultural feedlots, are far greater in volume. After they have entered the water, organic wastes begin to be broken down into their component parts by the action of bacteria. This process uses up dissolved oxygen in the water. The principal quantitative measure, therefore, of organic wastes is expressed in terms of biochemical oxygen demand (BOD). BOD measures the amount of dissolved oxygen that would be depleted by a specified quantity of the organic waste in a given time (usually five days) at a standard temperature (usually 20° centigrade). The degradable pollution content of various kinds of organic wastes can be commonly expressed in terms of the number of pounds of BOD they contain. All the higher forms of life in watercourses are aerobic—that is, they require free oxygen for life. As oxygen falls, they successively die—more sensitive fish, such as trout, first, and finally even the aerobic bacteria. When the latter go, the watercourse becomes "anaerobic" and its ecology changes drastically. The water becomes black and bubbly, and it stinks.

When BOD enters a stream, biological action begins to break it down and starts to use up the stream's oxygen in the process. Aeration of the water, through its interface with the air, restores oxygen. In general a sluggish stream absorbs less oxygen than a turbulent one and so restores its original oxygen more slowly. Moreover, the higher the temperature of the water the less oxygen it can absorb by aeration and the faster the bacteria will use up the dissolved oxygen. Electric utilities and other industries that use water as a coolant and discharge heated water back into the stream therefore cause thermal pollution, which is also an oxygen-robbing phenomenon. Quite apart from its effect on dissolved oxygen, heated water can directly damage or destroy fish and other life in a stream, although it is also possible that, under some circumstances, discharge of warm water could correct a heat deficiency in a watercourse with beneficial results.

The dissolved oxygen content of a stream begins to fall at the point where BOD is discharged into the water. The sag in dissolved oxygen continues for some distance down the stream and then the curve turns up as the restorative effects of aeration take over. Given the initial quality of the receiving water, the same amount of BOD discharge will, of course, have a more serious effect when the stream flow is low than when it is high. There are marked seasonal variations, therefore, in the water quality of any stream subject to polluting discharges.

The deficiency of dissolved oxygen at any point in a stream depends in a complex way upon the amount of BOD discharged and a set of these other factors—the distance down stream from the discharge point, the relative turbulence of the stream flow beyond that point, the volume of water flow, and the temperature of the water brought about by the interaction of climate and thermal discharges.

Among the products of the degradation of organic material are plant nutrients, primarily nitrogen and phosphorus. In and of themselves these elements are not harmful to the watercourse, but when present in excessive amounts they can lead to intense algae "blooms" which, in general, are damaging. This is particularly a problem in quiet waters such as lakes, bays, and estuaries. The process of excessive enrichment by plant nutrients is called "eutrophication."

If the source of the organic waste discharge is municipal sewage, the bacteria, viruses, and other biota it contains can be dangerous to human health. While purification systems avert this danger in municipal water supplies, the accumulation of organic wastes raises the costs of purification, and renders the receiving stream itself unfit for swimming and the like.

BOD serves as a good indicator of one aspect of pollution—the degradable residuals. But many residuals are *nondegradable*. These materials, which are mostly of industrial and agricultural origin, are not attacked by stream biota and undergo at most very little change once they get into a watercourse. In other words, the stream does not purify itself of them. They include inorganic substances—such materials as inorganic colloidal matter, ordinary salt, and the salts of numerous heavy metals. When these substances are present in fairly large quantities, they result in toxicity, unpleasant taste, hardness, and—especially when chlorides are present—corrosion. These residuals can be a public health problem, usually when they enter into food chains. Two particularly vicious instances of poisoning by heavy metals—mercury poisoning through eating contaminated fish (Minamata disease) and cadmium poisoning through eating contaminated rice (Itai Itai disease)—have stirred the population of Japan. Several hundred people have been affected and more than a hundred have died. The consumption of fish caught in certain locations has been restricted in many parts of the world, including North America, due to their heavy metal content.[1]

The third group of pollutants, mostly of relatively recent origin, does not fit comfortably into either the degradable or nondegrad-

1. There is some ambiguity in the degradable-nondegradable classification. The bacterial conversion of inorganic mercury to organic mercury is the cause of the mercury-associated public health problems. The same may apply to cadmium.

able categories. These *persistent* materials are best exemplified by the synthetic organic chemicals, such as some of the pesticides and related substances—especially the chlorinated hydrocarbons—produced in profusion by the modern chemical industry. They enter watercourses as effluents from industrial operations and also as waste residuals from household and agricultural uses. These substances are termed "persistent" because stream biota cannot effectively attack their complex molecular chains. Some degradation does take place, but usually so slowly that the persistents travel long distances, in streams and in groundwater, in virtually unchanged form. Due to their long life, some of them can be "magnified" in food chains, just as nondegradables like heavy metals frequently are.

Air Pollution

Each year factories, electric utilities, motor vehicles, homes, and incinerators in the United States pump hundreds of millions of tons of harmful pollutants into the atmosphere. In some ways, air pollution poses even more difficult problems of control than does water pollution. Since motor vehicles account for roughly half of the air pollutants (by weight if not necessarily by harmfulness), the polluting sources number in the millions rather than in the tens of thousands. The spread of pollution through the atmosphere and the associated effects on living things and on materials are fully as complex as they are in the case of water.

The principal pollutants emitted by motor vehicles are *carbon monoxide, hydrocarbons,* and *nitrogen oxides.* In heavy traffic, concentrations of carbon monoxide can build up to the point of danger to human health, particularly for people who suffer from heart disease and emphysema. Hydrocarbons and nitrogen oxides react with sunlight to produce smog, which corrodes materials, irritates the eyes, and, more seriously, engenders respiratory diseases and poses acute danger to those already suffering from chronic heart or lung disease.

Stationary sources—factories, utilities, incinerators, and some industrial processes—also emit large volumes of the smog-producing hydrocarbons and nitrogen oxides. The burning of coal and oil, principally for space heating or electricity generation, is the main source of large volumes of health- and property-damaging *sulfur oxides* and *particulates* in the air. Particulates contain not only inert materials but also heavy metals and other biologically active components.

The effect of a given quantity of emissions on the quality of the air depends on meteorological conditions and on the concentration of the emissions. Through dispersal, chemical reactions, and precipitation, the air can eventually cleanse itself of most pollutants. Light traffic on country roads or smoke from scattered rural factories does not perceptibly lower the quality of the air. But on a hot sunny day with little wind, rush-hour traffic and industrial emissions generate smog with its unpleasant, unhealthy, and even dangerous effects.

Water is delivered to us in pipes—we can treat it before we drink it, and overcome at least the most dangerous effects of water pollution. By contrast, our control over the atmosphere is very limited. Once we pollute the air we can do little about it: we must live in the polluted environment. Unlike people, however, fish did not create the pollution in which they must live.

Tracing Pollution to Its Source

Air movements and water flow carry residuals far from their original sources. At the same time, physical, chemical, and biological interactions take place between the residuals and the carrying medium. As a consequence, it is a very complex process to establish the relationship between environmental conditions in a particular location and the source of the waste discharges or emissions that caused those conditions.

Mathematical models have been developed that make it possible to determine the reduction in some types of pollutant emissions necessary to achieve desired improvements in "ambient" air and water quality. These models are virtually essential if policy makers, planners, and pollution control authorities are to plan and develop systematic and efficient control policies and programs. The models can, roughly at least, point to the reduction in sulfur oxide emission from fuel-burning plants necessary to reach a given level of air quality in a specific community; or to the cutback in BOD effluents from upstream factories and sewage systems required to upgrade the dissolved oxygen content of a river basin to some desired level.

Using mathematical models for such purposes is a feasible, but difficult, task. In the limited number of river basins or airsheds to

which they have been applied, however, these models have illumi-
nated the equity aspects, economic efficiency, and feasibility of
various control strategies. We make considerable use of the results
of such studies in chapter 7, where we present alternatives to the
control policies specified by present legislation.

In tracing the development of regulatory policy in the United
States, a very important distinction has to be made between the
setting of "ambient standards" for air or water quality and the
establishment of "effluent or emission limits" on particular sources
of pollutants. Ambient standards set targets for pollution-related
characteristics of the environment—for example, the amount of dissolved oxygen (in parts per million) along a stream segment.
Effluent or emission limits specify the amounts of a pollutant that
may be discharged from a particular source—for example, the
amount of BOD (in pounds per day) from a factory. Ambient
standards, taken by themselves, will represent no more than pious
wishes unless steps are taken, by one method or another, to ensure
that polluting sources limit the discharges that breach those standards. Initially, pollution control in the United States relied principally upon ambient standards for air and water quality, with the
federal and state governments assigned roles in detecting and moving against specific violators.

The difficulties of proving deviations from ambient environmental
standards, and of identifying the specific sources of pollution that
caused the deviations, make this kind of regulatory approach
virtually unenforceable. The recent legislation on air and water
quality shifts the emphasis by requiring the federal government to
set effluent or emission limits on specific sources of pollution. Chapters 3 and 4 trace this history and spell out its implications.

The Basic Economics of Pollution Control

The costs to the nation of controlling pollution will be large.
They will come in the form of higher prices, higher local taxes,
dislocation of existing plants, and alterations in life-styles and habits.
Inefficient control policies, which ignore the economic features of
the problem, can impose costs two or three times greater than is
really necessary. Because they are excessively expensive, poorly
designed policies can dilute political support for environmental improvement, stir hostility to control measures, and in the end add

ineffectiveness to inefficiency. We do not intend in this chapter to assess the policies and programs that have been undertaken in the United States. That is the task of later chapters. Here we explore a few basic economic propositions about pollution control that, when neglected—as they largely have been—can be major sources of inefficiency.

Design of efficient control policies requires attention to three basic facts about the economics of pollution.

1. The cost of reducing any type of pollution increases more than proportionally with the amount of pollution removed. In the economist's jargon, pollution removal, at high levels, is subject to increasing marginal costs.

2. The costs of pollution control vary substantially from industry to industry and from firm to firm. To be efficient, the degree by which individual sources have to reduce their pollutant discharges should vary in relationship to the cost of reduction. In reaching any given standard of air or water quality, the largest reductions should be made by pollution sources whose costs of control are least.

3. For almost every type of air and water pollutant there exists a large number of alternative control measures; the costs of these alternatives differ sharply, and the most efficient solution varies with the circumstances.

The following sections present a brief introductory discussion of these economic aspects of the pollution control problem.

Increasing Marginal Costs

As a virtually universal phenomenon, the greater the percentage of pollutants already removed from an industrial process, the higher will be the cost of removing an additional amount. This tendency has been confirmed by studies of numerous industries and different kinds of pollutants. For example, when 30 percent of the BOD has been removed from the waste discharges of a typical large meat-processing plant, the cost of removing an additional pound is 6 cents. But once 90 percent of the BOD is removed, another pound costs 60 cents; above 95 percent, the cost rises to 90 cents.[2]

The beet sugar industry also illustrates the exponentially rapid rise in costs as zero discharge is approached. The curve in figure

2. Ivars Gutmanis, "The Generation and Cost of Controlling Air, Water, and Solid Waste Pollution: 1970–2000" (Washington: National Planning Association, 1972; processed), Table 6.1, p. 162.

Figure 2-1. Marginal Cost of BOD Discharge Reduction by a Beet Sugar Refinery

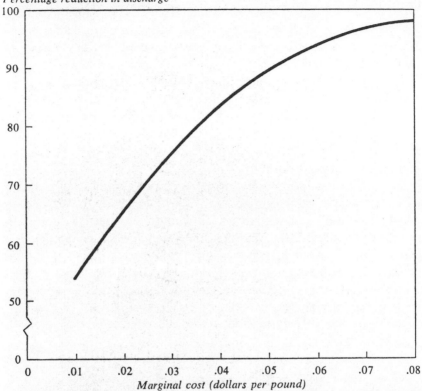

Percentage reduction in discharge

Marginal cost (dollars per pound)

Source: Clifford S. Russell, "Restraining Demand by Pricing Water With-drawals and Wastewater Disposal" (prepared for presentation at a seminar on the Management of Water Supplies, University of East Anglia, Norwich, England, March 1973; processed).

2-1 traces the increase in total costs associated with *each* successive unit of reduction. In the language of economists, this is a marginal cost curve.[3]

A petroleum refinery presents a similar picture in figure 2-2, demonstrating rapidly rising marginal cost as high levels of removal are approached.[4]

3. The least-cost combination of measures for achieving each level of reduction was used in deriving the costs.

4. See Clifford S. Russell, *Residuals Management in Industry: A Case Study of Petroleum Refining* (Johns Hopkins University Press for Resources for the Future, 1973). The fact that the curve for beet sugar manufacturing is continuous and that for petroleum refining is piece-wise linear is an artifact of the methods used to derive them. The petroleum case is based on a linear calculating model that takes account of restrictions on residuals discharge to other media.

Figure 2-2. Marginal Cost of BOD Discharge Reduction in Petroleum Refining

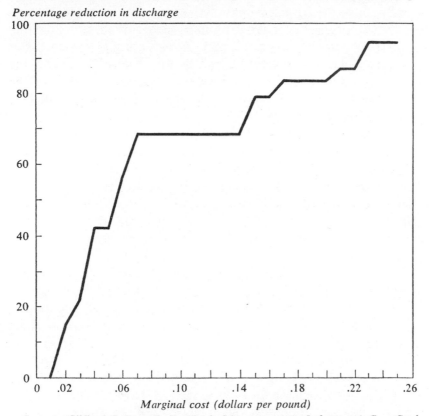

Percentage reduction in discharge

Marginal cost (dollars per pound)

Source: Clifford S. Russell, *Residuals Management in Industry: A Case Study of Petroleum Refining* (Johns Hopkins University Press for Resources for the Future, 1973).

The steep rise in incremental costs as pollution control objectives are raised has several implications. Depending upon the industry or pollutant, going from, say, 97 percent to 99 percent removal may cost as much as the entire effort of going from zero to 97 percent. In one analysis, the total ten-year cost of eliminating 85 to 90 percent of water pollution in the United States was estimated at $61 billion. Achieving 95 to 99 percent freedom from pollution would add *another* $58 billion, bringing total costs to $119 billion, or about 1 percent of national income. A 100 percent objective (zero discharge) would demand an *additional* $200 billion.[5]

5. Estimates prepared by the Environmental Protection Agency, the Council on Environmental Quality, and the Council of Economic Advisers, appearing as an exhibit in *Water Pollution Control Legislation—1971: H.R. 11896, H.R. 11895,*

The absolute values of these estimates should not be taken literally; there are so many unknowns—and thus so many assumptions—that precise estimates are impossible. In fact, a zero-discharge policy is probably a technical impossibility at any cost. But the central message is valid: although the costs of removing the bulk of pollution from the environment are modest relative to the size of the economy, the last few percentage points in pollution control objectives can involve huge costs.

These costs are not simply numbers for accountants or economists to ponder. They represent the value of the resources that must be channeled into controlling pollution and that will not be available for meeting the other wants of society. In the long run their principal source will not be the profits of industrial firms, but the higher prices and higher taxes that all of us will have to pay. Environmental goals therefore are not the simple consequence of decisions about how clean we want the air and water to be or how "tough" the government should be with particular industries. Establishing them confronts us, especially at the highest levels of control, with a set of hard choices between environmental quality and other aspects of living standards, in which the more we want of one, the less we can have of the other.

In addition, as control of one type of pollutant tightens, the need grows to convert the material for disposal to other media because of the principle of conservation of mass. Sewage sludge must be burned, airborne pollutants must be washed out of the gaseous stream with water, for two examples. Most cost estimates for high levels of control have grossly neglected these "intermedia" spillovers. As pollution control is pushed to ever higher levels, a coherent approach to the simultaneous management of the quality of all environmental media becomes critical. As a nation, we have yet to develop such an approach.

Differences in Pollution Control Costs

The examples cited in the preceding section illustrate another important fact about pollution control costs—they differ widely

---

Hearings before the House Committee on Public Works, 92 Cong. 1 sess. (1972), p. 259. The estimates combine the municipal and industrial costs shown in Tables II and III of the hearings exhibit.

from industry to industry. The incremental cost of removing pollutants above the 90 percent level is $0.05 per pound of BOD in beet sugar refining (figure 2-1) and $0.22 per pound for petroleum refining (figure 2-2). Even within the same industry, firms may face quite different costs of removing pollution; a firm that on normal economic grounds is about to set up a new production line may be able at little extra cost to redesign it to reduce pollution substantially, while another firm may have to incur much larger expense for redesigning a line already in existence.

These sharp differences in the cost of pollution removal among industries and firms underlie another significant conclusion about policy: the degree of pollution removal that each firm is required to make should take its costs into account. Suppose, for example, that the achievement of the desired level of dissolved oxygen in a particular river basin demanded a reduction of 90 percent in the amount of BOD entering the stream. Further assume that removing the last 1,000 pounds of BOD costs one firm in the basin 30 cents a pound, and another firm, in a different industry, only 5 cents a pound. The pollution control authority might impose a uniform reduction in BOD on each firm. But clearly the cost of achieving the 90 percent standard would be lower if the second (low-cost) firm were required to reduce pollution by a greater amount than the first. More generally, the total costs of control tend to be minimized by exacting the largest reductions in pollution from firms whose removal costs are least. Chapter 7 cites a number of specific studies that demonstrate that a "least cost" approach along the lines outlined above is far less expensive—by as much as 80 percent—than the uniform removal standard that has been the keystone of national policy until very recently.[6]

Alternative Control Techniques

There are usually a large number of different ways to improve air and water quality. These can be classified into four general types: (1) changing the way economic activity is carried out so that it generates less pollutants to begin with; (2) treating the pollutants as they emerge to render them less harmful; (3) increasing the capacity of the environment to absorb pollutants or changing dis-

6. See chapter 7 for an elaboration and justification of this point.

charge points in a way that does less damage to society; and (4) diverting pollutants to a different environmental medium (for example, from air to water, or from water to air).

In the case of water pollution, as the next two chapters demonstrate, government attention and policies have rested almost exclusively on the second approach—treatment of wastes already generated. But the range of other alternatives is very wide, and in many cases they embody cheaper or more effective ways of reducing water pollution. Firms can reduce the pollution they generate by modifying their production processes, switching to different raw materials, or changing the characteristics of what they produce. One study that gave close attention to these possibilities found that in beet sugar manufacturing, very great and efficient reduction of BOD discharge (one of the primary types of residuals from this type of enterprise) could be achieved by recycling and by-product recovery, and that only at the very highest level of control would "end of the pipe" treatment become economical.[7]

Steel presents another example of the influence of industrial process on the generation of residuals. Compared with the open hearth, the basic oxygen furnace (BOF) generates 45 percent more waterborne residuals (degradable organics, ammonia, solids, and heat), while the electric furnace generates virtually none.[8] The importance of process change has been observed in careful, detailed studies of pulp and paper manufacturing and food processing, and is no doubt characteristic of other industries as well.

Even more important than these examples of currently available technology is the strong influence economic incentives are known to have on the directions of technological inventions and their application to industries.[9] If private firms were adequately motivated

7. George O. G. Löf and Allen V. Kneese, *The Economics of Water Utilization in the Beet Sugar Industry* (Johns Hopkins University Press for Resources for the Future, 1968).

8. The differences arise because the BOF charge uses more hot metals than the open hearth and hence makes more use of the coke plant—the largest BOD source and the only source of phenols and ammonia; the electric furnace involves hardly any coking. See William J. Vaughan and Clifford S. Russell, "A Residuals Management Model of Integrated Iron and Steel Production" (paper presented at the Steel Industry Economics Seminar sponsored by the American Iron and Steel Institute and Northern Illinois University, DeKalb, Illinois, April 1973; processed). The steel-making technologies also have differential effects on other types of residuals. The significance of this is discussed below.

9. Jacob Schmookler, *Invention and Economic Growth* (Harvard University Press, 1966).

to modify their production processes so as to generate less pollution, there is every reason to believe that technology could be harnessed, in as yet unknown ways, to diminish rather than to increase pollution.

Water pollution can also be reduced by techniques that act directly on the watercourse. Water can be stored behind dams when the flow is high for release to dilute the concentration of pollution during low-flow periods. This technique of "low-flow augmentation" can sometimes be carried out by pumping ground water into the rivers or streams. Oxygen can be restored to the stream through large-scale aeration; and pollutants can be impounded in artificial lagoons and released gradually during periods of high flow. Alone, no one of these approaches will normally be sufficient to achieve reasonable control objectives. But as elements of a systematic approach to pollution control along an entire river basin, they can reduce the cost or increase the effectiveness of other control techniques. Indeed, for some types of water pollution, such as the runoff of wastes from agricultural feedlots, these may be the only feasible means of pollution abatement. We return to these alternatives in more detail in chapter 7. Here we wish merely to underline that they are real and important, and much neglected in national policy making.

So far at least, the atmosphere is not subject to manipulation by techniques analogous to low-flow augmentation or aeration. Air pollution emissions, therefore, must be controlled before they enter the environment. However, taking proper account of air pollution in designing urban transport systems (private vehicles versus mass transit) presents problems for planning and public investment analogous to those of river basin planning. Furthermore, in both air and water pollution control, land-use planning can sometimes be a useful tool for limiting the damaging effects of discharges and emissions from stationary sources.

In thinking about air pollution policy, it is useful to distinguish two kinds of polluting sources: mobile sources (primarily motor vehicles) and stationary sources (factories, incinerators, and the like).

Control of air pollution from automobiles can be approached in three principal ways: modifying the internal combustion engine and its exhaust system; adapting a radically different engine system which emits less pollutants; and controlling the amount of driving, especially in areas prone to smog.

Because the auto industry is dominated by the Big Three, a relatively small number of people will make the choice between the first two alternatives—modifying the gasoline engine or switching to a new type of propulsion. On the other hand, subject to whatever incentives and restrictions bear on them, the very large number of car owners will decide how much driving is done and where, and the extent to which engines and pollution control equipment are properly maintained. Policy approaches to this intricate problem are taken up in the following chapters. Suffice it to say here that current policy does not seem to be guiding us toward an optimal set of choices among the multitudinous options available.

Just as in the case of water pollution, stationary sources can reduce their pollutant emissions in a number of alternative ways. The emission of sulfur oxides from the combustion of fossil fuel, for example, can be reduced by switching to naturally low-sulfur coal or oil, by processing the coal or oil to remove some of its sulfur content, or by "scrubbing" the sulfur from the smoke stack. For any single firm the least expensive way to reduce sulfur emissions might be a switch to low-sulfur coal or oil. But since the supply of these fuels is limited, this cannot be the best solution for all firms.

In order to achieve environmental objectives at least cost, policy must somehow promote the adoption of those techniques of pollution control that are the most efficient in each case and simultaneously encourage the development and application of new technology. But since the least-cost combination varies from industry to industry, among firms within each industry, and among different locations, an approach allowing for a high degree of flexibility in response is needed. Current policy is, as we will see, rigid both in terms of specific requirements and in its view of technology. These are no trivial matters. Not only do hundreds of billions of dollars hang in the balance but also—so we believe—does the achievement, in the final analysis, of a high-quality environment.

Income Distribution

To an important extent the nation's economic and social structure has been conditioned by the fact that, historically, we have paid little attention to the problems of the environment. Goods and services have not commanded a price to cover the real environmental costs that their production and use imposed on society. As a consequence we have enjoyed cheap automobiles, paper, chemicals, food, energy, and a host of other products while suffering a deteriorated environment. Our standard of living, as conventionally measured, has to some extent been achieved at the price of dirty air and water.

However it is accomplished, cleaning up the environment will raise the cost of those goods and services whose production and use pollute the air and water. An efficient pollution control program will moderate the cost increases—but even then they will be substantial in some instances. The price of electricity will rise as utilities switch to the more expensive, low-sulfur, fuels or incur costs in removing the sulfur from their fuels. Motor vehicles with pollution control equipment will be more expensive to own and operate. In part, the costs of cleanup will resemble a series of excise taxes, with the heaviest taxes falling on goods whose production pollutes the most. Property taxes will also rise as municipalities construct and operate waste treatment plants. The costs of pollution control will be widely borne by individuals in their roles both as consumers and as taxpayers.

The period of adjustment to a cleaner environment will bring other kinds of costs. Some firms, finding that they simply cannot afford the cleanup, may have to go out of business. Some may be the major source of income for small communities; the town built around a small paper mill is an example. Ultimately, the economy can absorb the labor and capital thrown out of work by these adjustments, and various forms of assistance can be devised to ease the adjustment process. But a small fraction of the labor force and some local areas will necessarily sustain some painful transition costs.

The benefits of a cleaner environment will not be equally distributed. Those who live in distant suburbs or rural areas, for example, already enjoy clean air. But they will have to pay the higher prices for paper, automobiles, electricity, and other goods required to cover the expenses of reducing air pollution elsewhere. Those who live near the water, and those who enjoy the rivers or beaches for recreation, will gain more from the cleanup of water pollution than will those who live far from the river and those who vacation in the mountains.

Clearly, therefore, after the gains and costs of pollution control are shared out, not everyone will be affected equally. We have little basis for answering specific questions about the distribution of net benefits: Will the poor gain more or less than the rich? Will the central city resident benefit more than the suburbanite? Assuming that care is taken to minimize abrupt adjustment in local communities, it is unlikely that the achievement of reasonable environmental goals will drastically alter the distribution of income; both benefits and costs, while not equally shared, will be widely distributed. The fact that most of the costs of pollution control will be passed on in higher prices for a wide range of goods and services bought by the poor and by middle-income groups, however, does underline a point noted earlier. Devising efficient techniques of pollution control, so as to minimize the costs of achieving any given set of goals, should be a major aim of public policy. Otherwise, an unnecessary reduction in living standards will be forced upon many Americans who can ill afford to bear it.

Summary

This discussion has sought to lay the background for the subsequent five chapters which compare current pollution control policies, with their emphasis on regulation and construction subsidies, to an alternative approach relying on economic incentives and regional planning. Several facts about pollution control have been stressed:

• As environmental objectives become more ambitious, the cost of achieving them rises sharply, in terms of the other aspects of living standards that have to be sacrificed. The more rigorous the control standards, the more important it is that control policies be as efficient as possible in order to minimize those costs; and the more important it is that coherent and systematic policies with respect to all environmental media be developed simultaneously.

• Because the techniques and the costs of removing pollution vary widely from case to case, control policies that emphasize one particular technique or impose uniform limitations on all polluters are bound to be inefficient.

• A least-cost approach to environmental control requires the opportunity for complex discrimination among firms and among situations.

• An effective and efficient policy for controlling water pollution would in many cases include low-flow augmentation, stream aeration, and other kinds of public works. To plan, construct, and operate such large-scale projects, as part of a strategy for controlling pollution in a whole river basin, calls for regional control bodies. The same point applies with respect to air pollution in metropolitan regions in terms of planning urban transportation and land use.

• Because the costs of pollution control will be broadly shared, principally through higher prices for many widely bought goods and services, policy makers should vigorously seek an efficient set of pollution control techniques that hold costs to as low a level as possible.

CHAPTER THREE

Pre-1970 Federal Legislation and Its Problems

THE END of the sixties saw a greatly heightened interest in environmental matters and considerable disappointment with what had been achieved. The period therefore provided the context both for debate on next steps and for new legislation—on air pollution in 1970 and water pollution in 1972. Table 3-1 presents a chronology of the more important pieces of legislation, and an abbreviated account of their key provisions. A glance at the history of prior legislation is important, for it illuminates the origins of the new laws and some of the problems they may engender. We start with water, where experience is much richer; air pollution legislation, which followed a roughly similar pattern with a few years' lag, is taken up next.

Water

The first federal legislation dealing with the discharge of materials into the nation's waterways did not address pollution in any real sense. In an attempt to protect navigation, an obscure law, passed in 1899 as part of an appropriation act for construction and repair work on rivers, forbade discharge of any refuse matter (other than from municipal sources) into the nation's navigable waters without a permit from the Chief of the U.S. Engineers. This act (popularly known as the 1899 Refuse Act) was virtually unenforced until 1970;[1] after that it briefly assumed great prominence, and we will have more to say of it later.

Two minor pieces of legislation dealing with water pollution

1. Most permits issued were to contractors engaged in dredging and were related to the disposition of dredge spoils.

Table 3-1. Outline of Major Federal Legislation on Air and Water Pollution Control[a]

Date of enactment	Popular title and official citation	Key provisions
	Water	
March 3, 1899	1899 Refuse Act (30 Stat. 1152)	Required permit from Chief of Engineers for discharge of refuse into navigable waters.
June 30, 1948	Water Pollution Control Act (62 Stat. 1155)	Gave the federal government authority for investigations, research, and surveys; left primary responsibility for pollution control with the states.
July 9, 1956	Water Pollution Control Act Amendments of 1956 (70 Stat. 498)	Established federal policy for 1956–70 period. Provided (1) federal grants for construction of municipal water treatment plants; (2) complex procedure for federal enforcement actions against individual dischargers. (Some strengthening amendments enacted in 1961.)
October 2, 1965	Water Quality Act of 1965 (79 Stat. 903)	Sought to strengthen enforcement process; provided for federal approval of ambient standards on interstate waters. (Minor strengthening amendments enacted in 1966 and 1970.)
October 18, 1972	1972 Water Pollution Act Amendments (86 Stat. 816)	Set policy under which federal government now operates. Provided (1) federal establishment of effluent limits for individual sources of pollution; (2) issuance of discharge permits; (3) large increase in authorized grant funds for municipal waste treatment plants.
	Air	
July 14, 1955	1955 Air Pollution Control Act (69 Stat. 322)	Authorized, for the first time, a federal program of research, training, and demonstrations relating to air pollution control. (Extended for four years by amendments of 1959.)
December 17, 1963	Clean Air Act (77 Stat. 392)	Gave the federal government enforcement powers regarding air pollution, through enforcement conferences similar to 1956 approach for water pollution control.

Table 3-1 (*continued*)

Date of enactment	Popular title and official citation	Key provisions
October 20, 1965	Motor Vehicle Air Pollution Control Act (79 Stat. 992)	Added new authority to 1963 act, giving the Department of Health, Education, and Welfare power to prescribe emission standards for automobiles as soon as practicable.
November 21, 1967	Air Quality Act of 1967 (81 Stat. 485)	(1) Authorized HEW to oversee establishment of state standards for ambient air quality and of state implementation plans; (2) for the first time, set national standards for automobile emissions.
December 31, 1970	Clean Air Amendments of 1970 (84 Stat. 1676)	Sharply expanded the federal role in setting and enforcing standards for ambient air quality and established stringent new emission standards for automobiles.

a. The table covers only the important legislative enactments referred to in the text of chapters 3 and 4 of this book. It omits many amendments to the basic statutes that are not of major significance.

were enacted in the first quarter of this century.[2] But the first comprehensive federal legislation was the Water Pollution Control Act, passed in 1948 and amended a number of times since then.

The 1948 act is notable primarily because it was the federal government's first venture into what had been almost exclusively a state and local matter.[3] Its terms were, in fact, very weak and like all succeeding acts, it asserted that the primary responsibility for pollution control remained with the states; it gave the federal government authority mainly for investigations, research, and surveys.

The extensive amendments of 1956 embodied the strategy that dominated the federal water pollution program for the next decade and a half.[4] To be sure, amendments in that period made some changes. Federal authority was gradually extended and the ap-

2. These were the Public Health Service Act, 1912, and the Oil Pollution Act, 1924. Both have been virtually ignored in later discussions of the water pollution control program.

3. Exceptions were construction of sewers and activities for control of acid mine drainage by the Works Progress Administration in the 1930s.

4. The 1956 act is P.L. 84-660. Since that year, the 1948 act has been amended five times, in the following laws: Federal Water Pollution Control Act Amendments of 1961 (P.L. 87-88); Water Quality Act of 1965 (P.L. 89-234); Clean Water Restoration Act of 1966 (P.L. 89-753); Water Quality Improvement Act of 1970 (P.L. 91-224); and Federal Water Pollution Control Act Amendments of 1972 (P.L. 92-500). We will discuss the 1972 amendments in some detail in the next chapter.

proach modified somewhat. Also, the activity's locus within the federal bureaucracy shifted several times, in response to the shifting focus of interest in pollution matters: at first, interest in public health dictated placement of the enterprise under the Surgeon General; then, to elevate its status it was moved to the Office of the Secretary of Health, Education, and Welfare; the Federal Water Pollution Control Administration was created within HEW in 1965, but later was moved to the Department of the Interior as a means of emphasizing resource over medical concerns; and finally, in 1970, President Nixon moved the FWPCA into the new and independent Environmental Protection Agency, in order to integrate it with other environmental programs and to remove it from a department traditionally associated with resource development.

Two key elements in the 1956 amendments survived these modifications, and were to underlie the federal strategy until the early 1970s. The first was financial support for construction of waste treatment plants, which year by year involved higher levels of authorization and of federal contributions to individual projects. The 1966 act authorized $3.4 billion in grants for municipal sewage plants over the period 1968–71; but, just as they had under previous acts, subsequent appropriations of funds by the Congress ran below this rate. Municipalities could obtain federal grants to cover up to 55 percent of the costs of this type of construction, and private firms connected to municipal sewer systems could also benefit from the lower charges made possible by this subsidy. Furthermore, in the Tax Reform Act of 1969, as another method of subsidizing construction, Congress extended the tax advantage of accelerated depreciation to additions to industrial waste treatment plants.

The second key element of the 1956 amendments was federal regulation of waste discharge through enforcement actions against individual dischargers. Interstate polluters were the targets of these actions in their initial, weak form, but they were eventually widened to cover, in principle, virtually all sources of pollution, whether inter- or intrastate. In 1961 all navigable waters were included. One 1965 amendment permitted federal action if pollution hindered interstate commerce in shellfish. Others were intended, at least in part, to strengthen federal enforcement and to take account of regional differences in waste assimilative capacity and quality objectives. They gave each state the opportunity to present its own interstate water quality criteria, and implementation and enforcement plans, for review by the Secretary of the Interior. If states failed to do so, criteria and enforcement plans were to be promulgated by the secretary, subject to appeal. The development of state plans proceeded slowly and deadlines were missed by large margins.

Under these various acts the federal government apparently gained strong powers to bring enforcement proceedings against polluters. But these powers were used sparingly, for reasons to be explored subsequently.

Disenchantment with the Strategy

Although some students of the matter had argued for years that the strategy being evolved was profoundly defective, by the end of the sixties the growing disenchantment with programs for water pollution control had spread to many other quarters. For a long while, the tardiness, or total absence, of progress in the national effort was blamed mainly on underfinancing, changing laws, perpetual reorganizing, insufficient personnel for enforcement activities, and the like. But the strategy that was adopted suffered from much more fundamental deficiences. Three reports that became available in the early seventies highlight the character of these deficiencies and their relation to performance under the program. Two of these were by government agencies: a General Accounting Office study, referred to here as "the GAO report,"[5] and one in a series of reports by the Environmental Protection Agency, referred to as "Clean Water."[6] The third is by Ralph Nader's Task Force on Water Pollution, which we call "the Nader report."[7]

Federal Subsidies for Water Treatment Plant Construction

The first element in the federal strategy for water pollution control, which involves subsidies for construction, is often called an incentive program. Strictly speaking, that is a misapplication of the term, in its usual definition as that which incites to action. In the absence of other inducement, the mere availability of a subsidy will

5. Report to the Congress by the Comptroller General of the United States, "Examination into the Effectiveness of the Construction Grant Program for Abating, Controlling, and Preventing Water Pollution" (U.S. General Accounting Office, November 3, 1969; processed).

6. Environmental Protection Agency, Water Quality Office, "Cost of Clean Water" (EPA, March 1971; processed), two volumes.

7. David R. Zurick (ed.), *Water Wasteland* (Washington: Center for Study of Responsive Law, 1971).

not cause a municipality or an industry to reduce its waste discharge at all. Even though, say, half the cost of the treatment plant is paid for externally, it is still less costly to discharge the waste water untreated. Consequently, the subsidies must be linked in some fashion to the second element—enforcement actions against individual polluters—if the strategy is to be effective and coherent. As the GAO report documented, this integration was never realized, and the available federal grant funds were allocated on considerations other than the most cost-effective ways of reducing pollution of waterways. The beneficiaries were municipalities that for some reason were ready to act and the selection rested roughly on chronological priorities. In principle, the states were to establish priorities based on plans that promised the greatest improvement in water quality; hence, larger communities should have received the bulk of the available funds. But in practice, the funds went disproportionately to small towns that, however reluctant they might be to submit plans that entailed the commitment of their own funds, were more vulnerable to political pressures to apply for the subsidies.[8] Moreover, until the 1972 amendments, the maximum grant available to any one community was very small. In consequence, major metropolitan areas, whose rapid growth made their needs the most pressing, received little assistance. Table 3-2 reveals the lopsided allocation of grants arising from these policies.[9]

Because the allocations of federal funds under the grant program were essentially arbitrary from the point of view of economic efficiency, and were skewed toward smaller communities, the results were disappointing and costs were high. The program allocated funds among states according to a combination of state per capita income and population. As a result, funds were quite abundant in some states, and very sparse in others, relative to requirements. Where the funds were available, they were distributed within the state in accordance with its own priorities, which seldom had any relationship to an effective plan for cleaning up pollution along river basins. State priority lists contained communities that were "ready to proceed"

8. A study by the consulting firm of Camp, Dresser & McKee, reported in Appendix I of the GAO report, provided evidence that tying priorities to comprehensive plans could yield substantial benefits. It applied a system analysis to the Merrimack River basin and found that large cost savings were possible in a planned program of water quality improvement.

9. The law required that one-half of the grant funds go to smaller communities, and there was a ceiling on the total grant which may have discouraged some large cities from even applying.

Table 3-2. Distribution of Federal Water Pollution Control Act Grants and of Population, by Size of Community, January 31, 1969

Size of community	Amount of grants (millions of dollars)	Percentage of grants	Percentage of urban population, 1960ᵃ
Less than 2,500	173.1	15.3	0.6
2,500– 5,000	128.1	11.3	6.5
5,000– 10,000	155.9	13.7	8.5
10,000– 25,000	215.7	19.0	15.2
25,000– 50,000	150.6	13.3	12.9
50,000–125,000	143.9	12.7	} 22.1
125,000–250,000	62.5	5.5	
250,000–500,000	36.2	3.2	9.3
Over 500,000	68.8	6.1	24.8
Total	1,134.8	100.0	100.0

Sources: Grant distribution from U.S. Department of the Interior, Federal Water Pollution Control Administration, *The Economics of Clean Water*, Vol. 1: *Detailed Analysis* (1970), p. 110. Population distribution calculated from data in U.S. Bureau of the Census, *Statistical Abstract of the United States, 1968*, p. 16. Figures are rounded and may not add to totals.
a. Excludes 6.5 percent of urban residents not classified by population of city of residence.

—the ones that state authorities could bludgeon into building new or improved facilities. The situation was well outlined in the 1968 State of Maryland program plan:

Almost without exception, every sewerage project in Maryland has been undertaken at the suggestion, urging, insistence, formal orders, and, when administrative procedures are exhausted, by court action initiated by the Health Department and the Board of Health and Mental Hygiene. . . .
They build only what they are forced to build and only then if there are Federal and State grants immediately available. . . .[10]

The FWPCA pointed out that most states treated applicants on a first-come, first-served, basis, in a situation in which bargaining power prevailed and in which the bargaining units with the most power were often the largest polluters.[11] As a result of this approach, many urgently needed plants that would have substantially improved water quality were not built, while marginal plants were.

Furthermore, where large funds were available, their abundance tended to reinforce the inclination of local officials grossly to over-design public works in order to minimize appeals to the electorate

10. Quoted in U.S. Department of the Interior, Federal Water Pollution Control Administration, *The Economics of Clean Water*, Vol. 1: *Detailed Analysis* (1970), p. 116.
11. Ibid.

for authorization of bond issues. As a result of this tendency and of uncertainty on the part of local officials about the permanence of the subsidy program, fully one-quarter of the waste treatment capacity of metropolitan areas was less than half utilized while another one-sixth was overloaded.[12] This situation graphically illustrates the difficulty of devising subsidy schemes that do not themselves generate substantial biases toward inefficiency.

Another excellent illustration of this difficulty is provided by a limitation on the tax write-off provisions for industry. This benefit, which is still in effect, is withheld from a recycling process that permits recovery of salable or internally reusable materials. The intent of this limitation is obvious—the Congress did not want to provide a subsidy for new investment that would be profitable on its own. But the resulting bias against recycling is highly undesirable.

An additional shortcoming of the subsidy program was its emphasis on the construction of waste treatment plants and its virtually total neglect of their operation. This meant that a plant could be put on line and then operated, without penalty, far below its capability. Similarly, plants could be overloaded, so as to diminish the effect of treatment, without any public body taking adequate notice or having effective recourse. The philosophy appears to have been that once a treatment plant is built the problem is solved.

The most fundamental objection to subsidy arrangements, however, is that they do nothing to remove the perverse incentives with respect to the use of common-property assets like watercourses. They do nothing to bring the private costs of production into line with the costs to society, which include the environmental damages done to other users of the watercourse. They do nothing to mitigate the excessive generation of wastes—especially industrial and commercial wastes—in the first place. They generally ignore all methods for managing water quality other than conventional treatment.

In brief, the intricate problem of linking subsidies to enforcement was not solved at all; the subsidies were linked to the use of a particular technology—waste treatment—even in the frequent instances when other, more efficient, approaches were available; neither effectiveness nor efficiency played a role in allocating grant funds to particular communities; attention was focused on the con-

12. "Clean Water," Vol. 2, p. 72.

struction of treatment facilities and not their operation; and nothing was done to change the economic incentive to overuse and misuse common-property assets.

Finally, Congress periodically increased the share of construction costs eligible for federal grants and raised the authorized size of the grant program. But administration budgets and subsequent congressional appropriations consistently failed to provide the funds necessary to carry out these liberalizing actions. Local governments tended to wait for appropriations to be available before undertaking construction. As a consequence of these delays, some observers believe, the net result of the federal subsidy program was to slow down the effort to control water pollution.[13]

The Enforcement Program

The second element in the national strategy that developed in the 1956–72 period, the enforcement program, displayed shortcomings as grave as those in the subsidy program. The Water Pollution Control Act Amendments of 1956 established the "enforcement conference" as the keystone of the effort, and so it remained until the 1972 amendments. The administrator of the Environmental Protection Agency (EPA)[14] *could* call an enforcement conference to deal with an interstate problem; or the administrator could be requested to do so by the governor of a state with an intrastate problem if an interstate watercourse was involved. But with this sole exception, a conference was called purely at the administrator's discretion.[15]

The Nader report described the conferences and possible follow-up aptly:

These are purely informal convocations, marketplaces of pollution control ideas, from which the conferees are supposed to issue advisory recommendations to the Administrator of EPA. When "official" cleanup recommendations are adopted by the Administrator, who may or may not heed the suggestions of the conferees, they are purely exhortatory

13. For corroborating evidence, see *Environmental Quality: The Fourth Annual Report of the Council on Environmental Quality* (1973), p. 88.

14. The statutory authority for enforcement has always belonged to the official with overall administrative responsibility for the federal pollution program: the Surgeon General of the U.S. Public Health Service until 1961, the Secretary of HEW until 1966, and the Secretary of the Interior until the December 1970 reorganization that created EPA.

15. In 1961 the law extended to the governing body of any municipality the authority to request that a conference be called, provided that it could obtain the concurrence of the governor and of the water pollution control agency in its state.

and have no force as law. After a minimum period of six months has elapsed, the Administrator—again at his complete discretion . . .—may go on to the next stage of the conference procedure by convening a Hearing Board. The deliberations of the Hearing Board are formal but nevertheless result in yet another set of "recommendations." Another period of six months must elapse before the Administrator may—once again, this is discretionary—invoke the third and final stage of the conference procedure. He may ask the U.S. Attorney General (who presumably could exercise his own discretion and refuse) to initiate injunctive proceedings in Federal court to abate the pollution.[16]

The Water Quality Act of 1965 endeavored to shortcut some of this lengthy and cumbersome process by establishing standards for ambient water quality on interstate waters, along with an implementation plan. Logically, under the regulatory approach to enforcement, these plans should have incorporated specific limits on effluent discharges by the municipalities and firms along the watercourse, designed to achieve the stream standards. In practice the plans were vague, and relied principally upon a requirement that all effluent be subjected to secondary treatment or its equivalent (which removes 80 to 95 percent of BOD and 85 percent of suspended solids). As a general proposition, enforcing the law against individual polluters was difficult, because it would have been hard to provide legally acceptable proof that the actions of a particular polluter had caused a deterioration of stream standards. Indeed, the Nader report concluded that because the lines between ambient stream standards and effluent requirements were so weak, the requirements placed upon individual waste dischargers were almost certainly unenforceable at law.[17] By the end of the sixties it was becoming clear that, to be enforceable, the regulations would somehow have to establish effluent limits on each polluter.

In 1970 the federal government rediscovered the provision of the 1899 act that prohibited the discharge of wastes into navigable waterways by industry without a permit issued by the Chief of Engineers. Under prodding from Rep. Henry S. Reuss, of Wisconsin, the corps began to enforce the law; it received 20,000 applications for permits in eighteen months. A few permits were issued, but it was unclear how

16. The Nader report, Vol. 1, pp. VI-4, VI-5.
17. Ibid., Vol. 2, p. XIV-19. Support for this point of view is provided by a memorandum prepared for the Chamber of Commerce of the United States by the law firm of Covington and Burling, "Water Quality Standards under the Federal Water Pollution Control Act" (April 4, 1968; processed).

they would relate to the ambient standards and implementation schedules the states were laboriously establishing. In its 1971 report, the Council on Environmental Quality (the President's advisory body on environmental matters) emphasized the help the Refuse Act could lend in enforcement actions. But appeal of permit requirements to the courts mooted the issue.[18] Furthermore, while these court cases tended to focus on procedural matters, the use of an act, clearly intended by Congress to protect navigation, to prevent pollution probably could not have withstood further legal onslaught.

Experience under the Strategy

What has been the experience under the subsidy-enforcement strategy? A coherent discussion of accomplishments and failures is severely hampered by the lack of systematic data. Accordingly, the presentation is unavoidably anecdotal.

One way of examining effectiveness is to ask how, and how frequently, enforcement provisions have been used. During the fifteen years between the establishment of the enforcement conference procedure by the 1956 amendments and its review by the Nader task force in 1971, the federal government initiated official conferences on sixty different pollution problems, most of them on its own initiative on interstate waters. The vast majority of watercourses in the United States have never been considered in such a conference. None of the conferences has ever been officially "closed." Many have been reconvened several times over the years to consider new information, or to review progress; for example, the Conference on the Potomac has been reconvened nine times. In only four instances did the government stop the conversation and proceed to the hearing board stage. In only one has the process run its full course to a legal proceeding: in a suit brought against St. Joseph, Missouri, full compliance has yet to be achieved. Given the difficulty of establishing a connection between water quality standards and the actions of specific polluters under stringent judicial rules of evidence, the unimpressive record of legal enforcement is hardly surprising.

The enforcement conferences did produce some results. Forcing the waste dischargers and state agencies to make public statements,

18. The first and perhaps most important of these cases was *Kalur* v. *Resor*, decided in December 1971 by the U.S. District Court for the District of Columbia. The plaintiffs argued that the corps must issue an environmental impact statement under the new National Environmental Policy Act of 1969. The court upheld this view and the corps abandoned its effort.

and giving advocates of cleaner water a forum, has often stirred some action by the dischargers. To reinforce this influence, the conferences have usually been conducted with maximum publicity. But the whole process, from the selection of problem situations and of sources of wastewater to be discussed through the arrival at some sort of consensus, was highly vulnerable to political manipulations and delaying tactics.[19] Moreover, it tended to lose credibility because the enforcement procedures were practically never invoked.

Waste dischargers typically expressed good intentions in these proceedings, and then dragged their feet and delayed, sometimes for many years. Delays were beneficial from their narrow point of view, because they incurred no penalty whatsoever for delay in establishing a schedule or in adhering to it. Moreover, delays often allowed a waste discharger to obtain federal subsidies or to qualify for more favorable terms. The probability of an eventual court order was virtually nil, and in most instances the worst that could happen was a reconvening of the conference and further exposure to public scrutiny.

Another obstacle faced by the enforcement officials was their almost complete dependence on the residuals dischargers themselves for information about dumpings into the watercourses and about the options and costs for reducing them. This meant not only that they frequently needed to depend on shrewdly selected, if not totally inaccurate, information, but that to get any at all they had to cultivate the waste dischargers whom they were allegedly regulating. At the conference stage it was not possible to force the waste dischargers to divulge any information.

Experience with the shellfish clause, which apparently gave the administrator so much discretion, was no more inspiring. The clause could have been invoked on at least 427 occasions but was in fact used only 5 times.[20]

At the close of the decade, considerable use was made of a feature of the 1965 act that permitted the administrator to take violators of approved interstate standards to court on 180 days' notice, thus bypassing the conference procedure. Although a number of well-publicized notices were issued against cities, the usual result

19. Chapter 8 of the Nader report, entitled "With a Little Help from Their Friends," provides case studies of this process. Another illuminating case study is reported in Alexander Polikoff, "The Interlake Affair," *Washington Monthly*, Vol. 3 (March 1971), pp. 7–16.
20. The Nader report, Vol. 1, p. VI-16.

was also a conference. The main difference was that if the cities did not live up to their word, the administrator could go to the courts directly rather than waiting for the state to act, and several fines were levied. As we have seen, the flurry of enforcement actions in the early years of the Nixon administration, mostly based on the 1899 Refuse Act, became moot in 1972.

What Was Accomplished?

Perhaps a more telling standard for the efficacy of the national effort at water pollution control is its accomplishments in the control of the discharge of residuals and in improving the quality of watercourses. Although data are now being collected, judgment at present must rest on ridiculously gross estimates. Considering only point sources of BOD, and excluding storm runoff, EPA has estimated that U.S. industry generated 36 billion pounds of BOD in 1968, and the sewered population 8.5 billion pounds.[21] Municipal treatment plants removed two-thirds of the BOD generated by the sewered municipal population[22] but only 11 percent of industrial BOD generated. (During this period, industry discharged about 20 percent of its total wasteload to municipal plants.) The subsidized construction of municipal waste treatment plants can therefore have only a relatively modest influence on the discharge of industrial wastes.[23]

According to the Council on Environmental Quality, between 1957 and 1970, government subsidies of about $1.5 billion were provided for 10,000 waste treatment plants costing in total about $6.5 billion.[24] Over this period the number of people served by some kind of waste treatment rose 51 million. But this gain was mostly canceled by sewered population growth of about 36 million.

21. Point sources of wastewater are those that feed into the receiving watercourse in a pipe or confined channel. Nearly all industrial and municipal wastewaters are of this nature, although some urban storm water runs off directly to watercourses rather than through the sewer system. Some agricultural sources are also point sources; large feedlots and broiler houses are examples.

Nonpoint sources are those whose wastes reach the watercourse in a more diffused fashion. Storm water from farmlands, which often bears sediment and nutrients, and sediment-bearing water from construction activities are important examples.

22. Two-thirds of the U.S. population is served by sewer systems.

23. Data are from Clean Water, Vol. 2, p. 12.

24. *Environmental Quality: The First Annual Report of the Council on Environmental Quality, August 1970*, p. 46.

Moreover, as already noted, not only do some observers doubt that the federal subsidy program accelerated the construction of waste treatment plants; some believe that it actually slowed the process. Per capita expenditures in constant dollars have been just about level for the past fourteen years and dipped during the late sixties.[25] Quite possibly there would be a greater degree of treatment of municipal wastes today had the federal subsidy program never been instituted.

Moreover these figures relate only to the construction of treatment plants. Another GAO report issued in 1970 confirmed the long-held belief that existing plants were often operated poorly. Over half of the plants studied provided substandard service, either because they were badly operated or because they were not designed to treat the waste load delivered to them. This is not really surprising, since the federal program emphasized construction exclusively; there were no incentives to spur effective and efficient operation.

The GAO report recounts events in some basins where dramatic growth in industrial discharges overwhelmed whatever progress had been made in municipal treatment. These are spectacular instances, and across the country residuals discharges have not grown so dramatically. The authors of "Clean Water" estimated the change between 1957 and 1968 in two types of residuals discharge, BOD and one plant nutrient (phosphorus). Estimates of the former are built on the 1968 calculations mentioned earlier, and suggest that discharge of BOD increased a little less than 10 percent; plant nutrients (from point sources only) about doubled.[26] The authors admit that their estimates are extremely crude, especially in the case of industry; and their effort must be deemed heroic in view of the almost total ignorance about the generation of industrial residuals and about the amount of treatment performed after generation. Even given the rough assumption about facilities in place, the estimate of discharge is suspect, we feel, because it is based on the doubtful assumption that industrial treatment facilities are operated very effectively. But if the estimate of a spectacular doubling of industrial BOD *generation* between 1957 and 1968—a period during which industrial production as a whole grew only about 60 percent—is anywhere near

25. See Council on Environmental Quality, *Fourth Annual Report* (1973), p. 88.
26. See "Clean Water," Vol. 2, pp. 29, 34.

accurate, it offers a striking illustration of the failure of the present treatment-oriented policies to discourage *generation* of residuals in the first place.

The GAO report concludes, and it is not difficult to agree, that underfinancing of federal programs, and scattershot assistance unrelated to systematic plans for improving water quality, largely canceled the effectiveness of the federal program.

Lack of Attention to Institution Building

In our view a crucial failure in the policy strategy developed after World War II is the neglect of institution building. As we shall discuss later in more detail, substantial economic-engineering research during the decade of the sixties made a compelling case for the systematic management of entire river basins using a wide array of technologies in addition to the control of discharges at individual outfalls.[27] Furthermore, for the major nonpoint sources of residuals, such as agricultural land, logging areas, and urban storm runoff, large-scale regional measures to improve land use and enlarge the assimilative capacity of streams may be the only practical ways to achieve better water quality. Federal legislation during the period under consideration embodied virtually no support for the development of regional river-basin agencies, which could have planned and put in place demonstrably effective and efficient technologies reaching beyond controls at individual points of wastewater discharge. Providing the only support for regional planning and institution building available from the federal government, the 1956 amendments to the Federal Water Pollution Control Act set up planning grants to states and regional agencies to develop coherent approaches to the problem. In later years expenditures under this program ran about $2 million a year—virtually nothing; they represent about 0.2 percent of the subsidies for construction of treatment plants. Moreover, planning was generally separated from any institutional mechanism for implementation. Thus for reasons of both scale and organization, little came of these efforts.

Even accepting the bias in the grant program toward treatment relative to other technologies, the requirement that grants be made in such a way as to contribute to a comprehensive program de-

---

27. A summary can be found in Allen V. Kneese and Blair T. Bower, *Managing Water Quality: Economics, Technology, Institutions* (Johns Hopkins Press for Resources for the Future, 1968).

veloped by state authorities could have encouraged a more effective use of funds. Perhaps resulting "comprehensive plans" could have laid a foundation for genuine regional management approaches in the future. But as we have seen, in practice, this requirement was mainly lip service.

In the longer perspective—especially in light of the relationship between the management of water quantity on the one hand and the need to develop programs for control of the residuals from nonpoint sources on the other—the failure to build institutions that could undertake efficient region-wide management was perhaps the most profound deficiency of the entire approach.

Concluding Comment on Water

Federal efforts in the water pollution area during the past fifteen years undoubtedly focused national attention on the problem and put pressure on state and local governments and industry to take some steps toward environmental cleanup. The specific design of federal policy, however, clearly hampered effective action. Assessments of why the reality failed to match the intent of the laws will differ. But by the end of the 1960s many persons interested in water quality were deeply disappointed and felt a need for something new. This feeling was fueled by the great upsurge of environmentalism and by several public and private reports severely critical of the old approach. The GAO and Nader reports are excellent examples, but there were also at least implied criticisms forthcoming from various professional communities as well. In the minds of the congressional committee members dealing with water pollution, the major problems seemed to be a shortage of funds to build waste treatment plants and the lack of federally imposed effluent limits on individual polluters.

It was in this atmosphere that the administration and the Public Works Committees of Congress set about in 1971 and 1972 trying to put the water pollution effort on a new course. The final outcome of this effort was the 1972 amendments to the FWPCA. We will turn to these in the next chapter.

Air Pollution Legislation through 1967

In origin and progress, federal air pollution legislation has followed much the same route as the water pollution legislation we have just tracked, but with a lag of several years. The major exception to this generalization arises from the fact that much of the overall air pollution problem is attributable to the products of a single giant oligopolistic industry—automobiles. Indeed, it was a combination of Los Angeles smog and an acute episode of industrial pollution in Donora, Pennsylvania, in October 1948, causing some twenty deaths and about six thousand illnesses, that stimulated the process out of which finally came the Clean Air Amendments of 1970.

In 1950 researchers at the California Institute of Technology established a link between automobile emissions and photochemical smog in the Los Angeles Basin. A short time later the Los Angeles Air Pollution Control District began calling for action from the automobile companies and the state government. Despite company claims that the requisite technology was not available, a study group was set up under the auspices of the Automobile Manufacturers Association and reached a cross-licensing agreement for emission control devices. Over the same period a number of resolutions were introduced in the Congress, though not passed, calling for federally sponsored research on the air pollution problem. Senators Thomas H. Kuchel of California and Homer E. Capehart of Indiana took a leading role in this new effort; in 1955 Senator Kuchel introduced legislation authorizing a federal program of research, training, and demonstrations. In the meantime President Eisenhower had received a report from an interdepartmental study committee recommending the same steps. Congress passed the legislation and the President signed the first federal law on air pollution in July 1955.[28] The level of activity authorized by the 1955 Air Pollution Control Act, however, was very low—$5 million annually for five years to support all its functions.

By this time the problem in California had worsened, and the state took the initiative in establishing automobile emission controls. A new law requiring recirculation of crankcase blow-by (reducing hydrocarbons by about 20 percent) on new 1963 cars induced the industry to begin installing the simple crankcase device on some 1961 models. In 1963, over the objection of the automobile industry that such technology did not exist, California legislation required exhaust control devices on vehicles once two such devices were approved by the State Motor Vehicle Control Board.

28. P.L. 84-159.

When four devices produced by independent manufacturers were approved in 1964, the industry discovered that it could indeed introduce its own devices on cars sold in California starting with the 1966 model year. In that year the first California emission standards were set.

Meanwhile, back in Washington, nothing much happened for quite a while. The main reason was that air pollution was widely regarded as an exclusively state and local problem, as exemplified by the official position of the Department of Health, Education, and Welfare toward the 1955 act. Accordingly, eight years elapsed between this act and the first permanent air pollution legislation, although in 1959, the 1955 act was extended for four more years.

In 1962 President Kennedy asked the House to pass a bill sponsored by Senator Kuchel that had passed the Senate in 1961. It authorized the Surgeon General to hold hearings on particular interstate air pollution problems. Some features relating to the research program and grants to state and local governments were added. The House again deferred action. Meanwhile, another major incident, a deadly smog that hit London in the winter of 1962, underlined the dangers of air pollution.

A recommendation by the administration in February 1963 finally produced the Clean Air Act, signed by President Johnson in December of that year. This law for the first time gave the federal government enforcement powers. They followed closely the pattern of the procedures earlier legislated for water pollution. At the request of a state, HEW could call a conference on air pollution problems in a particular region or airshed; then hold hearings; and if no satisfactory result followed, finally bring court action. In interstate cases, HEW could act on its own initiative. The bill also specifically mentioned the need for additional attention to the auto exhaust problem.

Hearings held in 1964 by the Senate Public Works Subcommittee on Air and Water Pollution underlined the inadequate attention that had been given to automobile emissions in federal legislation. The administration held that voluntary cooperation should be sought from the industry, and so it opposed enforcement legislation proposed by Senator Edmund S. Muskie of Maine in 1965. But this position was widely denounced in the press, leading to a reversal by the administration. Thus a second title to the 1963 act was passed

in 1965 as the Motor Vehicle Air Pollution Control Act authorizing
HEW to set emission standards for automobiles as soon as practicable.[29] The first standards were for 1968 models and were
roughly the same as those applied in California in 1966. Many
people felt that the federal program was unimaginative and lagged
behind the progressive California program.

Exacerbating the matter, the automobile industry took a series
of bewildering actions that destroyed—almost as if intentionally
—the favorable public image that it had so long held. The attempt
by General Motors to intimidate Ralph Nader backfired spectac-
ularly, and its president was forced to apologize before a congressional committee and a national television audience. During the
same period the Los Angeles County Board of Supervisors charged
that the Automobile Manufacturers Association committee, established ostensibly to exchange emission control information, was
really a setting for collusion to prevent or delay controls. They cited
evidence and asked the attorney general to take action. The ensu-
ing Justice Department investigation ended in 1969 with a consent
decree providing for an end to possible conspiratorial activities
while not officially conceding their existence. The year before,
representatives of the industry had given testimony on alternatives
to the internal combustion engine which, to put it mildly, was highly
deceptive.[30] The image of the industry had hit rock bottom. These
events contributed heavily to the political climate in which the 1970
act was passed.

The 1967 Air Quality Act

In the move toward control of air pollution, a dramatic incident
once again proved to be a factor. A four-day inversion episode in
New York in 1966 was estimated to have caused eighty deaths.
A month later a National Air Pollution Conference was held, which
HEW hoped to use as a stimulus to new legislation embodying
regional control organizations and national emission standards.
Senator Muskie, Chairman of the Pollution Subcommittee at that

29. P.L. 89-272.
30. *Automobile Steam Engine and Other External Combustion Engines,* Joint
Hearings before the Senate Committee on Commerce and the Subcommittee on
Public Works, 90 Cong. 2 sess (1968).

time, conceded that stronger legislation was needed but opposed national standards. In 1967 President Johnson delivered a message to Congress dealing primarily with air pollution matters and, despite Muskie's opposition, proposed legislation including national emission standards for major industrial sources and establishment of regional air quality commissions for enforcement.

After hearings that reinforced Senator Muskie's reluctance about national emission standards, the Senate Public Works Committee delayed a decision, and reported a bill that provided for a two-year study of such standards and that transformed the regional agencies from devices to enforce them into organizations involved with the states in setting them. The pattern of the 1965 Water Quality Act was followed. HEW was charged with issuing "criteria" which set forth the relationship of concentrations of specific pollutants in the atmosphere to damages to "health and welfare." Ninety days after publication of the criteria, each state had to file a letter of intent that within six months it would establish standards for ambient air quality and, within six more months, implementation plans for each of those pollutants in the airsheds over which it had jurisdiction. The secretary of HEW could establish such standards himself if the state failed to comply. The final version, which left these elements intact, was passed and signed by the President in November 1967 as the Air Quality Act.[31] The act also authorized a greatly expanded research effort and for the first time set national standards for automobile emissions.

Thus at the end of 1967 the federal law pertaining to the setting and enforcement of air pollution standards for nonmobile sources had roughly the same structure as water pollution legislation had attained in 1965. It was not long before this approach came under severe fire.

Experience with the enforcement conference process was similar to that in water pollution, perhaps even worse. Between 1963, when the process was initiated, and 1970, eleven conferences were initiated, all but one on interstate cases. Only one case was heard by the courts; it concerned a rendering plant in Bishop, Maryland. Most of the other enforcement conferences included the whole of

31. P.L. 90-148.

major metropolitan areas and their recommendations dealt largely with desirable organizational arrangements. These anticipated the requirements under the 1967 act.

Furthermore, HEW was slow to provide the criteria that were the first step in the state-regional approach dictated by the act, and the states in turn were slow to act once criteria were issued. By 1970 not a single state had a full-scale plan of standards and implementation in effect for any of the pollutants, and a Nader study estimated that the process would not be concluded until well into the 1980s.[32] This report not only roundly condemned HEW's National Air Pollution Control Administration and all its works but also contained an attack on the Subcommittee on Public Works. Other senators and committees were trying to push into the environmental arena. And the President boarded the now fast-rolling environmental bandwagon. Nineteen-seventy was the year of Earth Day. The credibility of the automobile industry was shattered. This was the dramatic political setting for the Clean Air Amendments of 1970,[33] to which we now turn.

32. John C. Esposito (ed.), *Vanishing Air,* The Ralph Nader Study Group Report on Air Pollution (Grossman for the Center for the Study of Responsive Law, 1970), p. 158. An informative discussion of enforcement problems in the air pollution field is found in *Assessment of Federal and State Enforcement Efforts to Control Air Pollution from Stationary Sources,* Report to the Congress by the Comptroller General of the United States (U.S. General Accounting Office, 1973).

33. P.L. 91-604.

CHAPTER FOUR

The Present Laws

FOR REASONS made obvious in the preceding chapter, the end of the 1960s saw widespread dissatisfaction with the strategy for pollution control that the federal government had laid down during the previous decade and a half. Moreover, there was no clear evidence that pollution was being reduced on a broad national scale. Progress made in some areas and on some substances was more than canceled overall by population and economic growth. The time appeared ripe for reconsideration of what, to many, was an irreparably defective approach. Nevertheless, in the major laws of the early 1970s, Congress chose to push ever harder the approaches that relied on regulation and on construction subsidies. Hard-line regulation and enforcement were the main themes of the 1970 legislation on air pollution.

The 1970 Clean Air Amendments

The 1970 Clean Air Amendments sharply expanded the federal role in setting and enforcing standards for ambient air quality, and greatly tightened emission limitations on motor vehicle pollutants. With respect to the first, the act embodies the concept of a "threshold" value—a level of ambient concentration below which it is assumed that no damage occurs to health. Materials subsequently designated to have threshold values include the main pollutants by mass (sulfur dioxide, carbon monoxide, nitrogen oxides, particulates, and oxidants). The notion of threshold value can be regarded as a politically convenient fiction which permits the law to appear to require pollution damage to be reduced to zero—an absolutely unambiguous number.

Congress directed the Environmental Protection Agency to use scientific evidence to determine threshold values for pollutants assumed to have them, and then to set those values minus "an adequate margin of safety" as "primary standards." These standards, which relate to injury to human health, are to be met first. More rigorous standards, to be met later, relate to public "welfare" and aim to protect property, crops, livestock, and public transportation from pollutants. The states were to prepare implementation plans assuring that the primary standards would not be violated anywhere in the state after mid-1975. These plans to meet primary standards were supposed to have been completed by the beginning of 1972; deadlines for the secondary standards were more flexible.

The Congress did not rely solely upon the establishment of standards for ambient air quality to control pollution. It also gave the EPA power to set specific limits on the emission of certain kinds of pollutants. It recognized a category of substances called "hazardous pollutants," which are considered to have especially serious health implications (some of the heavy metals are examples). The EPA was directed to prepare a list of such substances and to issue regulations limiting their emissions by both new and existing sources, which were to be enforced at the federal level.

The act also directed the administrator to set "new source performance standards," which limit the emission of pollutants from new industrial plants to an amount no greater than attainable with "the best adequately demonstrated control technology."

Perhaps the most striking feature of the new legislation was in the amendments to the National Emission Standards Act (Title II of the Air Quality Act of 1967), which established specific emission standards for automobiles. These include limits on hydrocarbons (HC) and carbon monoxide (CO) for new model cars in 1975 and an additional standard for oxides of nitrogen (NO_x) to be met in 1976.[1] They aim at a 90 percent reduction from 1970 levels for HC and CO and from the 1971 level for NO_x. Since large reductions had already been achieved in the former in 1970, the act effectively calls for a 97 percent reduction, compared with uncontrolled conditions.[2] This degree of reduction was justified as insurance that ambient concentrations of pollutants would remain below those associated with adverse

1. As we will see in chapters 5 and 6, the 1975 and 1976 requirements have now been relaxed.
2. Expressed in grams per mile (gm/mi), the standards were determined to be 0.41 HC, 3.4 CO, and 0.04 NOx.

health effects. As enforcement mechanisms, EPA is to carry out compliance tests, establish fuel regulations, and require and enforce performance warranties from manufacturers. The enormous $10,000 fine per vehicle for violations illustrates the symbolic "get tough" aspect of the act since its imposition on more than a small proportion of vehicles would surely have no other effect than to halt automobile production. As has been pointed out elsewhere, "the overall tone of the legislation is that of an impatient Congress forcing a reluctant administrator and a resisting industry to act promptly."[3]

In the next two chapters, we will have some words to say about the objectives and implementation of the act.

The 1972 Water Pollution Control Act Amendments

By the end of the sixties, the relevant committees of the Congress recognized that the water pollution program that had emerged from earlier legislation not only was not working well but probably was unworkable. Also, the administration had been urging the Congress to overhaul the Federal Water Pollution Control Act to put it on a different track. Accordingly, the Senate and House in November 1971 and March 1972, respectively, passed comprehensive water quality bills as amendments to the 1956 act. A conference committee version was passed by both houses but was vetoed by the President, primarily on grounds of the burden on the federal treasury. Congress promptly and overwhelmingly overrode the veto.

Two national goals are set forth in the opening section of the 1972 act: (1) ". . . that the discharge of pollutants into the navigable waters be eliminated by 1985"; and (2) ". . . that wherever attainable, an interim goal of water quality which provides for the protection and propagation of fish, shellfish, and wildlife and provides for recreation in and on the water be achieved by July 1, 1983."

Several of the innovations, implicitly or explicitly, embodied points proposed by the President:

• Extension of the federal-state program to all navigable waters within the United States.

• Effluent standards for individual plants that discharge water-

3. Henry D. Jacoby, John Steinbruner, and others, "Federal Policy on Automotive Emissions Control" (Harvard University, Environmental Systems Program, March 1973; processed), p. 13.

borne wastes and, under different criteria, standards for publicly
owned waste treatment plants.

• Mandatory use in new facilities of the best available and
economically achievable technology for pollution control.

• Stringent federal standards for toxic discharges.

• A permit system for discharges from industrial and municipal
waste dischargers (thereby incorporating into the pollution laws the
permit provisions that had been included in the old 1899 Refuse Act
as a means of keeping the navigable water free of refuse).

• Stronger and more streamlined federal enforcement procedures
tied into the effluent standards and permit systems.

• Heavier fines on violations, from $2,500 to $25,000 a day for
a first offense and up to $50,000 a day for subsequent conviction.

• Provisions by which citizens can bring legal actions to enforce
standards.

• Self-sufficient municipal financing of treatment plants after the
current backlog of municipal needs has been met.

The older enforcement strategy, which generally required that a
connection be shown between standards of ambient water quality
and the discharges of a specific polluter, was thus replaced by a
delegation of power to the central authorities to impose effluent
limits directly on individual waste dischargers and to issue permits
based on those limits. The permit system includes municipal treatment plants and industrial establishments. While the permits can be
issued by states whose criteria and procedures have received federal
approval, the Environmental Protection Agency is empowered to
veto any individual permit that it considers unwarranted.

More emphasis is also placed on research, demonstration, and
education, including work in basin planning and area-wide treatment systems, though the sums involved remain quite modest.[4] (If
one took seriously the goal of zero discharge by 1985, much of this
would be irrelevant anyway.) Another striking feature of the 1972
amendments is the heavier stress they place upon matching federal
grants for construction of publicly owned waste treatment plants.
Such grants, as we pointed out in the last chapter, have long been
part of the program; recently they have amounted to about $1 bil-
lion a year. The new legislation raises the maximum federal contri-

4. Moreover, the requirements for plans as a condition for the receipt of federal subsidies are tough and cumbersome and have greatly limited the capacity of
EPA to commit subsidy funds.

bution from 55 to 75 percent of total costs, and authorizes up to $5 billion in grants for the fiscal year 1973, $6 billion for 1974, and $7 billion for 1975. In addition, it authorizes up to $2.75 billion for retroactive payments to certain localities that previously constructed facilities without federal assistance.

The subsidy authorizations clearly are what prompted the President's veto of a bill that contained so many of his recommendations. Unlike most authorizations, these did not require subsequent appropriation in a separate congressional action.

In the process of enacting the 1972 amendments, the Senate and House initially passed separate bills which, on some points, had important differences. The foremost among these were the procedure for establishing effluent limitations and the degree of federal intervention in the issuance of individual permits once the state permit programs had been approved. On the first issue the Senate bill depended on levels of available technology ("best practicable" technology by 1976 and "best available" by 1981) with a no-discharge policy to take effect by 1985. Accepting the 1976 goal, the House bill deferred action on the 1981 and 1985 goals until the National Academy of Sciences and Engineering had made a comprehensive study of the economic, social, and environmental effects of both achieving and not achieving the goals. Even then action could be taken only if authorized by a law passed after the submission of the academy's report. Unlike the Senate version, the House bill also would have allowed EPA to grant a two-year extension of the 1976 deadline to individual dischargers under certain narrow conditions.

On the second issue, the Senate bill allowed federal veto of individual permits issued by states within approved programs, while the House bill gave the states more latitude on the matter. The compromise submitted by the conference committee followed the Senate version in most essential respects.

The ultimate act retained the feasibility study, but assigned it to a new National Study Commission,

which shall make a full and complete investigation and study of all of the technological aspects of achieving, and all aspects of the total economic, social, and environmental effects of achieving or not achieving, the effluent limitations and goals set forth for 1983 . . .[5]

5. P.L. 92-500 (86 Stat. 875). The conference version moved the 1976 goal to 1977 and the 1981 goal to 1983.

The commission was given a three-year life from date of passage (October 1972) and $15 million to do its work. It was to be composed of fifteen members, five each from the Senate and House Public Works Committees, and five appointed by the President. Thus, two-thirds of the members of the body charged with evaluating the feasibility of the goals set in the act are members of the committees that drafted it.[6]

Accounts of the considerations occupying the Public Works Committees and their staffs as they framed the legislation do not suggest that cost and efficiency were major considerations. But in late summer 1972, the chairman of the Senate committee, Senator Muskie, did raise substantial reservations about a proposal on grounds of its heavy cost.[7] This was in response to an earlier proposal by Senator Tunney that all the nation's waterways be made fit for swimming and the propagation of fish, shellfish, and other wildlife by 1980. Nevertheless, despite Senator Muskie's concerns, the committee went on to design a bill with cost implications that, as we will see in chapter 6, were more severe at that time than those thought to be associated with the Tunney proposal.

Why did this happen? We address the general reasons underlying this sort of outcome in the epilogue. But in this case there apparently were two special reasons. One was the fear by those senators and representatives who considered themselves defenders of the environment that they would suddenly be outdone by someone proposing completely clean air or pure water. After all, how could they be caught settling for "slightly dirty" water?

The other factor seems to have been dedicated and highly effec-

6. The Congress had good reasons for fearing an appraisal by the professional community, for opinions emanating from that quarter have been harsh. At a conference in late 1972, James Coulter, long a scientist and administrator in the water quality field, first with the federal government and then as Secretary of the Maryland Department of Natural Resources, said: "I will make no attempt to convince you that the water pollution control act passed by Congress is ridiculous. That it is a silly law is a matter of record. If you wished to, you could pick the law up and read it. I know that these are damning words to the Congress of the United States. After all . . . this law passed the Senate with an overwhelming majority of 74 to 0 and some 366 to 11 in the House. Knowing how complicated the language is and how tough it is to read, I am wondering if the vote does not merely reveal that eleven Congressmen read the act." C. W. Cook and others, *Environmental Management Guidelines for Policy,* Presentations of an Invitational Meeting, 1972 (University of Texas, College of Engineering and Lyndon B. Johnson School of Public Affairs, no date), p. 19.

7. As reported by the *National Journal* (January 15, 1972), p. 88.

tive work by a small number of conservationists advocating zero discharge. They seem to have felt that the more stringent the restrictions were, the cleaner the water would be, although there is absolutely no historical justification for this view.[8] The committee staff never seriously sought information on alternative strategies despite strong advocacy by many prominent individuals and institutions.

With some exceptions, industry was neither vigorous nor effective in opposing the legislation or in helping to shape it, deterred perhaps by its apparent inevitability or by its apparent ineffectuality. Despite qualms among staff people in agencies concerned with water quality management and despite some notable voices raised in dissent, the states went along, mostly because they did not want to be labeled dirty-water advocates and because they wanted the federal money. As we will see in chapter 6, the act, if taken literally, represents a pronounced shift in national priorities. It is a shift never carefully analyzed during the framing of the legislation, and it takes costs far beyond even the scale that seems to have worried Senator Muskie at one stage of the hearings.[9]

8. It brings to mind the situation in the Ruhr region before the creation of the well-known river-basin associations (Genossenschaften), which succeeded in developing an effective and efficient water quality system for the region. Things got so bad that at one point the desperate authorities ordered the city of Essen to stop discharging any effluent. Thereupon the Bürgermeister is said to have remarked, "We now have no choice but to wall up the main sewer and drown in our own effluvium."

Before the reform of water legislation in the late sixties, French law called for essentially zero discharge and specified severe penalties for violations. The result was that the law was never enforced because its unreasonableness was apparent to all concerned. Consequently, nothing was done to control water pollution.

9. The congressional committee staffs appear to have given little consideration to the interrelationships between the water environment and other media. We treat this matter in chapter 7, which outlines a coherent policy approach to the whole problem of residual materials.

CHAPTER FIVE

Enforcement Problems

THE 1970 and 1972 legislation set very ambitious goals for environmental control. Reaching the targets set forth in these acts raises two major questions: first, how effectively can the requirements of the legislation be enforced through the machinery of regulation and construction subsidies; and second, what would be the costs and the shift in national priorities if the targets were achieved? This chapter looks at the problems of enforcement; the next deals with costs.

Technology and the Clean Air Amendments

One of the main tools by which the Clean Air Amendments of 1970 aspire to improve air quality is the requirement laid on the Environmental Protection Agency to set performance standards in the form of emission limits on newly constructed stationary sources of air pollution. These limits are to be based not on air quality standards but on what EPA deems to be the best "adequately demonstrated" technology for reducing emissions. The Federal Water Pollution Control Act Amendments of 1972, which aim at reducing and eventually eliminating discharges of water pollutants, rely upon the same techniques. EPA is charged with developing and enforcing effluent limitations for point sources, and eventually nonpoint sources, based on its judgments about technological feasibility, subject to a vaguely defined test of "reasonable" economic costs.

It is therefore worthwhile to look briefly at the experience with this technology-based approach under the Clean Air Act and to examine its implications for water quality control.[1] The legal issues

1. A useful discussion of the enforcement problems associated with the Clean Air Amendments is found in Noel de Nevers, "Enforcing the Clean Air Act of 1970," *Scientific American*, Vol. 228 (June 1973), pp. 14–21.

that have already arisen in connection with the new-source provisions of the amendments to the Clean Air Act are probably symptomatic of those that will arise in connection with the setting of standards for wastewater effluents, although the latter promise to be even more complex because of the greater diversity of water uses and of control technologies. We then discuss in detail the massive efforts now under way to lay the basis for enforcement of the restrictions in the water quality act, and subsequently return to the problem of automotive emissions and state plans for air pollution control in metropolitan areas.

The group in EPA responsible for issuing new-source performance standards chose to deal first with electric power plants, municipal incinerators fired by fossil fuels, and plants that make sulfuric acid, nitric acid, and cement. In all of these industries, emission control involves comparatively straightforward, if not unquestionably effective, technologies.

The standards have been issued and are now in contention. In the case of power plants, the major issue revolves around what constitutes adequately demonstrated technology for controlling sulfur dioxide (SO_x) emissions. The EPA points to several plants built three decades ago in England and Japan with equipment for controlling sulfur oxides that is available in the United States today, while the industry contends that the equipment is unreliable and expensive to operate. The issue is in the courts.

In early September 1973, EPA softened its rules on SO_x emissions from power plants and smelters by permitting tall smoke stacks for dilution. Such stacks lower the concentration of pollutants, because they are mixed with a greater volume of air before they reach ground level; but the area affected is greater. Acting EPA Administrator John R. Quarles, Jr., exposed the unhappy dilemma in the present legalistic approach when he said the choices were "this or nothing or a shutdown" of plants that could not meet the EPA standards.[2]

In setting standards for cement plants, EPA found that some were removing more fine particulates than was any electric power plant. It therefore issued a more stringent standard for cement plants than for electric power plants. This move is also being chal-

2. *Washington Post,* September 7, 1973.

lenged in court because it seems to penalize the more innovative industry.

Three critical provisions of the 1972 amendments govern the establishment of effluent standards for water quality control.[3]

First, a 1977 deadline is set for achieving "effluent limitations for point sources, other than publicly owned treatment works, . . . which shall require the application of the best practicable control technology currently available . . . ." This has been called the best-practicable-technology (BPT) standard.

Second, a 1983 deadline is set for achieving "effluent limitations for categories and classes of point sources, other than publicly owned treatment works, which . . . shall require application of the best available technology economically achievable for such category or class, which will result in reasonable further progress toward the national goal of eliminating the discharge of all pollutants . . . such effluent limitations shall require the elimination of discharges of all pollutants if the Administrator finds . . . that such elimination is technologically and economically achievable for a category or class of point sources. . . ." This has been called the best-available-technology (BAT) standard.

Third, in establishing guidelines for BPT and BAT, EPA is charged to take into account "the age of equipment and facilities involved, the process employed, the engineering aspects of the application of various types of control techniques, process changes, non-water quality environmental impact (including energy requirements), and such other factors as the Administrator deems appropriate . . . ." In addition, in determining BPT, but not BAT, the administrator is to consider "the total cost of application of technology in relation to the effluent reduction benefits . . . ." The use of the term "economically achievable" in the BAT definition, however, does introduce similar economic considerations.[4]

3. Actually the Congress provided not only for the establishment of effluent limitations based on technological factors, but also for limitations based on ambient water quality. In a given body of water, if the limitations based on technological considerations resulted in ambient water quality inferior to that called for in established water quality standards, the limitations would have to be tightened. Apparently, however, the Congress intended that the technologically based limitations become the primary mechanism of control, and we will focus on that. In actuality, it is quite possible that, because of court cases and other pressures, national standards for best practicable technology and best available technology will be forced toward the lowest level of acceptable practice. In that case, water quality standards would, at least in principle, come to govern.

4. 86 Stat. 845 and 851.

EPA has announced that for the time being it will concentrate on the 1977 standards in its permit-issuing activities.[5] This is perhaps logical enough, and is dictated by the terms of the 1972 law, out given the durability of equipment, and the fact that the two deadlines are very close together, the industrial manager should know both requirements to plan his investment efficiently. Moreover, the optimum path toward achieving "best available" in 1983 may not lie through the "best practicable" point in 1977, a possibility that opens another intriguing avenue of disputation.

Requirements for both BPT (1977) and BAT (1983) raise the issue of what is "economically achievable." The BAT requirement does so explicitly and the BPT requirement implicitly, with its reliance on "practicable" and with its reference to the weighing of costs and benefits. Furthermore both requirements are vague about whether the administrator, in setting actual standards as contrasted to guidelines, must consider each plant separately or may deal with categories and classes of plants.[6]

Representative Robert E. Jones, a member of the House subcommittee dealing with pollution control, seems to have made the only congressional statement on this issue when he remarked that "when the term 'economic capability' is referred to, it means the economic capability of the given point source."[7] He also pointed out that "the term 'total cost of application of technology' . . . is meant to include those internal, or plant, costs sustained by the owner or operator and those external costs such as potential unemployment, dislocation, and rural area economic development sustained by the

5. The bureaucratic process actually going on is complex and not exactly consistent with the legislation; furthermore, it reflects internal disagreement in EPA. The Effluent Guidelines Division and its contractors are developing the definitions of BPT (1977) and BAT (1983) without reference to water quality. Once the guidelines have been developed, the enforcement division is to utilize them in actually issuing permits.

Late in 1973 a federal court order (resulting from a suit brought by an environmentalist group) required EPA to add a number of industries to the list for which it was preparing guidelines, and to tighten deadlines. For the group EPA had already been working on, final promulgation of guidelines was to be finished by October 1, 1974—a two-month tightening of the schedule EPA had defined. This caused concern in EPA about whether the quality of work will deteriorate and therefore result in guidelines that will not hold water—so to speak. An account can be found in *Air and Water News*, Vol. 7 (December 17, 1973), pp. 1–3.

6. In this discussion we draw some of our information from a particularly useful paper by Robert J. Rauch, "The Role of Technology Assessment in the New Water Pollution Control Law" (Harvard Law School, March 15, 1973; processed).

7. *Congressional Record*, daily ed., October 4, 1972, p. H9117.

community, area, or region."[8] Clearly, these considerations can be pertinent to specific cases, and if taken literally would imply tailoring effluent standards individually to virtually every plant in the nation. The language of the act that requires the administrator to consider the age of equipment and facilities also suggests that within industries standards can be varied according to the vintages of plants.

On the other hand, there is evidence that other members of Congress, including Senator Muskie, intended a very limited role for such differentiation, and hoped for nationally uniform effluent standards. The report of the conference committee states: "The Administrator is expected to be precise in his guidelines . . . so as to assure that similar point sources with similar characteristics, regardless of their location or the nature of the water into which the discharge is made, will meet similar effluent limitations."[9]

One can't help but agree with Rauch that "it is sufficient to say that no definitive legislative interpretation of this section is possible."[10] There seems to us no realistic way for the administrator to

---

8. Ibid.
9. *Federal Water Pollution Control Act Amendments of 1972*, Conference Report, H. Rept. 92-1465, 92 Cong. 1 sess. (1972), p. 126. The EPA is implementing the section in three ways:
1. A task group is developing guidelines based on high performance actually achieved with attention solely to technological aspects. The work on specific industries is being done by EPA staff or through contracts with review by EPA. But while the contractor is supposed to search for exemplary technologies, he is also required to submit cost information on water effluent treatment, so as to allow EPA to develop cost effectiveness curves. The assessment of waste control possibilities is made by "categories of industry" which in principle could be sufficiently fine to include only a single plant. In practice they are broader, but still, in some cases, try to take account of significantly different circumstances of residuals generation. There is stress here between EPA and the industries, with the latter pressing for a larger number of categories to reflect the "uniqueness" of situations.
2. Another task group, also a combination of EPA personnel and contractors, is working on the whole range of possible economic impacts. The factors being considered and the procedures being followed are none too clear to an outsider, but the basic cost information apparently comes from the documents prepared under the auspices of the Guidelines Division.
3. The administrator, after considering the results of these activities, was to issue preliminary standards by October 1973 for the first twenty-seven industries. After response by interested parties, the final guidelines were to be promulgated four months later. As previously mentioned, a court decree resulted in a new schedule for guideline issuance.
10. Rauch, "Role of Technology Assessment." A legal analysis of the standards provision of the amendments is found in Robert Zener (Deputy General Counsel, Environmental Protection Agency), "The Federal Law of Water Pollution Control," in Erica Dolgin and Thomas Guilbert (eds.), *Federal Environmental Law*

avoid negotiating and bargaining with virtually every individual source of waste discharge of any size. Even then he would probably face a huge bureaucratic and legal task,[11] since some 33,000 plants have applied, and estimates of the total number of major sources run up to 55,000.[12] The result will almost surely be long delays, a capricious distribution of control efforts, and, to the extent the program succeeds, an extremely costly way of achieving water quality goals.

The difficulties in establishing the later BAT standards appear to be as troublesome as those for the earlier BPT ones. Futhermore, perverse incentives for innovation are inherent in framing requirements in this way. If "best available" is taken to mean the best equipment installed in any plant—the apparently logical interpretation and the one that seems to have been adopted—then such equipment would immediately become the standard for the industry. The interpretation could go further to include technology that has been developed but not yet implemented. But then who in industry would seek an innovation that added to costs, even if it sharply reduced pollution? From industry's standpoint, such innovations, because they are guaranteed to reduce profits, are to be shunned like the plague.

The 1985 zero-discharge goal strikes us as so unrealistic that it hardly deserves discussion. But we will take it up again in chapter 7,

---

(West for Environmental Law Institute, 1974). Zener finds that variances from uniform effluent standards may be given to individual point sources, but only for technical reasons having to do with their equipment. Differing economic circumstances, Zener finds, do not justify variant standards for individual sources.

11. An indication of what may be in store occurred at the 1973 International Pollution Control Engineering Exposition and Conference in Philadelphia, where an attorney specializing in environmental matters advised industry to take a page from the environmentalists' book and take EPA to the courts. In this connection he pointed to some recent court victories for industry on environmental matters and the shaky basis of EPA emission standards. An account can be found in *Air and Water News,* Vol. 7 (October 29, 1973), p. 1.

Even now, before the act has begun really to pinch, and early in the history of the legislation, severe, if predictable, problems abound. An excellent illustration is found in John R. Quarles, Jr., "Expectations Vs. Achievements: Some Reflections on the Water Act," U.S. Environmental Protection Agency, *Environmental News* (January 1974), pp. 2–16. After the usual statements about the monumental nature of the act, the article becomes a litany of administrative problems, deadlines unmet, and hopes dashed. Quarles concludes, "The cold, sober appraisal I promised you at the outset leads me to conclude, at this stage of the game, that it isn't going to happen the way many of us hoped it would" (p. 12).

12. If permits are issued by those states granted permit-issuing authority, they are still subject to review, and ultimate approval, by EPA.

where we consider a unified strategy for environmental management. Here we will simply note that one of its main failings is its disregard of the interdependencies among the various environmental media; for pushing control of water pollution to the zero-discharge level is almost certain to complicate control of air and solid waste pollution.

We are forced to conclude that the amendments may be no more enforceable than previous laws and that they carry a potential for gross inefficiencies in achieving environmental objectives in both the long run and the short run. Furthermore, they do little, if anything, to encourage arrangements for the enduring management of the problem on a coherent regional basis.

Automobile Emissions

In many urban areas the automobile is by far the largest source of deterioration in atmospheric quality. Clearly, strong action was needed, and in many respects the Congress is to be admired for attempting to subject to regulation an industry that in one way or another may account for more than one-tenth of the nation's gross national product. The tool it fashioned duplicates the tough enforcement mechanism just discussed with respect to water—tight deadlines and massive retaliation for not meeting them. In this case the club is a fine of $10,000 per vehicle for violating the 1975–76 standards.

On the one hand, the few firms and the highly standardized technology in the industry make enforcement easier here than in other pollution situations. On the other hand, its size and importance make its shutdown unthinkable. The analogy of the "nuclear deterrent" used by EPA Administrator William Ruckelshaus in commenting on the legislation is apt: it is a powerful weapon but no one in his right mind would use it short of an unavoidably catastrophic situation. Just why the automobile companies should comply in a full and timely fashion under these circumstances is not clear. Public relations seems to be the key.

The tight deadline, plus the resistance of the automobile industry to innovation, makes it realistically impossible to meet the established deadline in any way other than tinkering with the design of the conventional internal combustion engine. Even then, meeting the standards is not at all certain.[13] A number of careful studies have established that adapting the internal combustion engine is a poor way to achieve low levels of automotive emissions in the longer run. If left unaltered, however, the present law will almost certainly have the effect of freezing us into the standard internal combustion engine for a long time to come since it offers little incentive for the development of inherently low-emission alternatives like steam or turbine engines.

Controlling carbon monoxide (CO), oxides of nitrogen (NO_x), and hydrocarbons (HC) simultaneously to low levels is extremely difficult with the internal combustion engine. For technical reasons, control to low levels of CO and of HC tends to raise emissions of NO_x, and control to low levels of NO_x tends to raise CO and HC. Thus, a complicated system will be necessary to adapt the engine to meet the 1976 standards, which cover all three. The system will probably include exhaust recycling and two catalytic converters —one with an oxidizing catalyst for CO and HC, and one with a reducing catalyst for NO_x. Severe problems of low mileage, poor performance, and more expensive maintenance may follow, with the consumer bearing much of the cost. Furthermore, the system is so delicate that it may be badly damaged by such routine "hazards" as a fouled spark plug or running out of gas. The Jacoby report estimated these extra costs at perhaps $4 billion per year for initial installation, another $4 billion per year for fuel penalty and maintenance, and perhaps $1 billion per year for enforcement.

Maintenance problems are one of the causes of high enforcement costs, but not the only one. Because the optimum tuning of an adapted internal combustion engine differs according to whether it is aimed at fuel economy and performance or at emissions controls, the consumer has an incentive to reduce the effectiveness of his emission controls. Since the gases his vehicle emits are invisible, only tests can uncover misdirected tuning. And they will be bedeviled by the incentive to tune in one way for test purposes and subsequently in another for actual driving. In an effort to ease the

13. We treat the topic of automotive emission control rather briefly, because there is an excellent recent discussion available with which we are in almost total agreement. See Henry D. Jacoby, John Steinbruner, and others, "Federal Policy on Automotive Emissions Control" (Harvard University, Environmental Systems Program, March 1973; processed). A very useful discussion is also found in Lawrence J. White, "The Auto Pollution Muddle," *Public Interest*, No. 32 (Summer 1973), pp. 97–112.

situation temporarily, EPA has reduced its 1976 NO_x standards and delayed the more stringent standards until 1977.[14] Even so, the internal combustion engine, with its inherently high emissions and difficulties in control, appears to be here to stay for many years. The desirability of a power source with inherently low emissions, such as a stratified charge or steam engine, is obvious.

The present strategy will undoubtedly achieve a reduction in emissions. In a slightly longer-term perspective, however, this reduction will come about by inefficient, cumbersome, and generally troublesome means, and with much less promise of further improvement. A strategy that set less rigid deadlines, tried to deal specifically with some especially bad local situations, but provided incentives for phasing out the internal combustion engine would almost certainly have been preferable and more likely to achieve longer-run objectives. We outline the elements of one such strategy in chapter 7.

State Plans

The 1970 amendments required the states to submit control plans for existing stationary sources of "threshold" pollutants and for urban transportation that would assure that the national primary ambient standards were never exceeded in any part of the state after June 1975. Plans have been submitted by most states, but they will almost certainly fail to realize the objectives of the act.

One reason is the persistent problem that states have in making

14. Responding to requests from automobile manufacturers, EPA in the summer of 1973 relaxed the 1976 deadline for NO_x control, and established interim standards for that year. The auto makers claim they cannot meet even this standard. Since then, EPA has indicated that errors of measurement and technique may have led to an excessively strict NO_x standard; a National Academy of Sciences committee has been engaged to look broadly at the problem. A *Wall Street Journal* article of May 29, 1973, by Jude Wanniski, provides a good discussion of how the standards were set. EPA has now exhausted its delay privilege under the 1970 Clean Air Amendments. Further moves are up to Congress, and a bill providing further delays was being considered at the time of writing.

A new element entered the auto emission control picture late in 1973. The results of several tests showed that the catalyst designed to reduce hydrocarbon and carbon monoxide emissions may at the same time spew out unacceptable amounts of another dangerous pollutant, sulfuric acid. This could be the basis for a "technological backfire." See Deborah Shapley, "Auto Pollution: EPA Worrying That the Catalyst May Backfire," *Science*, Vol. 182 (October 26, 1973), pp. 368–71.

regulations stick against large industries.[15] In Arizona and Montana, two of the largest copper-producing states, the industry was able to subvert the presentation of a legally acceptable plan for control of sulfur oxides from smelters. Finally, EPA decided itself to issue regulations for all copper smelters. These regulations are now in litigation, and EPA is backing away from them.

Another problem arises because state plans typically call for the use of low-sulfur fuels—natural gas, and low-sulfur oil and coal—to comply with standards for emissions. Indeed, this is probably the only way that, given present energy demands, the standards could be met, in view of the still precarious state of the technology for controlling stack gas and the time needed to introduce it. However, confinement to low-sulfur fuels necessitates sharp reductions in the amount of coal used, especially in the East (where most coal has a high sulfur content), and, in compensation, very large increases in oil imports. In view of the oil embargo, the EPA administrator encouraged the states to relax some of their requirements, and pressures are mounting to relax them still further. Fuel switching forced by state regulation of sulfur content has, in fact, been responsible for nearly all of the improvement in air quality traceable to emissions of sulfur and particulates from stationary sources. In many ways this is a weak reed for improvement to lean on. The switch was not very costly when it took place, and thus not much resisted except by the coal industry; but now low-sulfur fuel is becoming drastically scarce. Since fuel switching does not embed major new technologies in the system (that's why it worked so quickly), it can readily be reversed, and there are strong signs that this is already happening.[16] If some enterprise can obtain a variance or an easing of the regulation, nothing keeps it from polluting in the same old way without any penalty whatsoever.

Possibly the most critical problem area in the state plans is urban transportation. In thirty-seven metropolitan areas especially affected

15. See, for example, the discussion of state enforcement in *Assessment of Federal and State Enforcement Efforts to Control Air Pollution from Stationary Sources,* Report to the Congress by the Comptroller General of the United States (U.S. General Accounting Office, 1973), pp. 7–22.

16. A staff report of the Federal Power Commission's Bureau of Power estimated that nearly one-half of the boilers that had been converted from coal to oil could be reconverted within three weeks; most of the rest could follow in due course. See "The Potential for Conversion of Oil-Fired and Gas-Fired Electric Generating Units to Use of Coal" (FPC, rev. November 1973; processed), p. 5.

by automotive emissions, the federal limits on emissions, even if achieved, will not by themselves reduce such pollutants sufficiently to meet the air quality standards by 1975. The pertinent states were, accordingly, required to include proposals to restrict transportation in their plans. Forty-three plans were submitted by twenty-three states for thirty-seven metropolitan areas. In June 1973 EPA announced its approvals of eight plans essentially as presented, and amended the others in various ways up to full-scale promulgation by the agency. By the end of July, transportation control plans were announced for thirty-six cities. In some cases their implications were modest, with little more needed than the contemplated reductions from stationary sources and in new-car emissions (the achievement of which is, however, dubious). Any additional reductions required could, in these cases, be achieved by inspection and maintenance requirements for automobiles, assuming the other control objectives were met. In other cases, parking restrictions and improved mass transit service were deemed sufficient supplements to the controls already discussed.

But these relatively simple procedures were thought to be adequate in only about ten cases. Others would call for heavy costs, like those involved in fitting catalytic converters to existing cars; or for broad forsaking of traditional behavior, like a 20 percent reduction in driving, with its massive implications for public transportation.

CHAPTER SIX

Economic, Budgetary, and Other Costs

WHEN CONGRESS initiates an interstate highway system, increases social security benefits, or authorizes a military weapons system, the costs of these actions appear in the federal budget. Although they often turn out to be much higher than originally estimated, costs are explicitly considered in the decision to undertake the program.

Environmental control programs are different. A large fraction of their costs will be borne not by the federal government but by individuals, in the form of more expensive electricity, fuel, paper, automobiles, and other goods and services, and by state and local taxpayers in higher costs for municipal waste treatment. Because their costs do not draw the attention that the budget can focus on the usual federal program, efficiency—that is, realizing a particular set of goals at least cost—is not a central concern in designing environmental control strategies. In fact, efficiency arguments are often dismissed as relatively unimportant; and very ambitious goals are set on little information or with little consideration of whether the benefits are worth the costs. We do not mean that ambitious goals should be forsworn. But setting such goals and designing programs to reach them without attention to costs are bound to make for bad public policy.

The 1970 and 1972 legislation on air and water quality set in motion federal programs broader than any previously undertaken in the domestic arena. Even now, let alone at the time the legislation was passed, no one knows the costs of achieving the environmental objectives established in the law. As we argued in the last chapter, intractable enforcement problems will almost certainly defeat the aims of these laws. In the early parts of this chapter, however, we will generally assume that they will be met, so that we may spell out some cost implications as clearly as possible. Statements that such and such "will" happen should be understood in this light.

In the case of water pollution control, not all of the standards set in the 1972 act have yet been translated into specific requirements for industry. But the costs will be very large. The National Water Commission (NWC) roughly estimated that between 1972 and 1983 the cumulative costs of meeting the requirement to use the best known technology[1] (not for zero discharge), set out in the 1972 water pollution amendments, will be $220 billion, leaving aside the difficult and potentially very costly problems of runoff from agricultural feedlots, acid mine drainage, and storm water discharges —the so-called nonpoint sources discussed below.[2] On the basis of data in the 1973 Report of the Council on Environmental Quality, the costs of reaching the air quality standards of the 1970 amendments may approach $135 billion to $140 billion over the same period. Together the two programs may cost some $375 billion in the 1972–85 period, and possibly half again as much if nonpoint sources and storm water discharges are included. Crude estimates would put the cost of achieving the less ambitious goals contained in earlier legislation at about $100 billion to $125 billion —a cost difference of at least $200 billion to $250 billion between the two sets of goals.

While the validity of these particular estimates is open to question, the 1970 and 1972 legislation incontrovertibly represented a national commitment of many hundreds of billions of dollars. Whatever its precise dimension, this is not a simple financial magnitude of interest to economists and accountants alone. As we pointed out in the second chapter, the dollar figures represent real resources of labor, capital, and raw materials devoted to pollution cleanup, which would otherwise have been available for building homes, educating children, constructing mass transit systems, building and

1. The commission's cost estimates based on "best known technology" are necessarily only a rough approximation of the cost of the "best available technology" required by the 1972 act in 1983, since EPA had not yet specified BAT when the estimates were made.
2. NWC estimates that meeting the problem caused by storm runoff in urban areas will cost an additional $248 billion. But no one has any idea of the best way to handle this problem, much less of its realistic costs.

maintaining vacation facilities, and the host of other goods and services bought by individual citizens and by federal, state, and local governments.

This chapter examines the various kinds of pollution control costs. It emphasizes two major points: the importance of designing efficient programs and the need to evaluate environmental goals in terms of costs. First, if costs over the next decade and a half approach $400 billion, even a 25 percent reduction—a modest estimate of the potential saving from careful design—would release $100 billion of resources for other purposes. Second, as chapter 2 pointed out, raising the goal for pollution removal from 95 to 99 percent adds far more to costs than the step between 91 and 95 percent. As a nation, we might be wise to take the last step. But surely, doing so is not sensible without explicitly weighing the environmental gains against the other goals we might achieve with the same resources.

In the most fundamental sense, we get the benefits of cleaner air and water by sacrificing other aspects of our living standards. While these sacrifices will take many forms, they will affect individual citizens in three major ways: (1) through the federal, state, and local taxes required to pay for municipal waste treatment plants; (2) through the higher prices charged by industries and utilities to cover the costs of meeting environmental standards; and (3) through the higher prices and annual operating costs for automobiles occasioned by air pollution control requirements.

Table 6-1 presents estimates of the capital and operating costs of achieving the interim standards of the 1972 act for municipal waste treatment. The estimates for dealing with urban storm runoff are extremely uncertain. In many major cities storm and sanitary waters run through the same sewers into waste treatment plants. During rainstorms the sudden surge in the volume of water exceeds the capacity of treatment plants, and raw sewage spills into the waterway. Separating storm from sanitary sewers would require massive capital outlays in most metropolitan areas. Even after separation, storm water, if not treated, would deposit large amounts of pollutants, like suspended and dissolved solids, biochemical oxygen demand (BOD), and metallic ions, into the waterways. Lagoons to hold the storm water for gradual feeding into treatment plants have been suggested as an alternative.[3] In any event, the appropriate techniques and the costs of dealing with this problem are highly uncertain, and the estimates in Table 6-1 should be viewed simply as indications of the exceedingly costly nature of the undertaking.

Under current law, the federal government pays 75 percent of the cost of constructing waste treatment plants. State and local taxpayers carry the remaining 25 percent and all of the operating costs. Of the $77 billion for construction and operating costs of municipal waste treatment shown in Table 6-1, the federal taxpayer thus would contribute about $35 billion and state and local taxpayers about $42 billion.

The estimates presented in the table are the costs of meeting the interim standards for municipal wastes laid down in the 1972 act, which require that secondary treatment be universally applied by 1977. To satisfy the more stringent standards set forth for 1983, municipalities would have to spend substantial additional amounts beginning several years before that date. Since the implications of the more stringent standards for municipalities have yet to be specified, however, the magnitudes of those additional costs cannot be estimated with any confidence.

Industrial Costs

The available estimates of industrial costs suffer from a number of defects. When the estimates were made, EPA had not yet precisely defined the "best practicable" and "best available" technology required in 1977 and 1983, respectively, under the water quality control amendments. Moreover, the estimates assume that many industries will meet the water pollution control requirements principally by treating their wastes, rather than by the often cheaper means of changing product design, switching raw materials, or modifying internal production processes. In its 1973 report, however, the Council on Environmental Quality did present estimates for industry (including utilities) of meeting the interim "best prac-

3. One of the problems with storm water is its content of small suspended particulates. These would not be predictably removed by standard sewage treatment processes, so at least part of the problem would remain.

Table 6-1. Estimated Capital and Operating Costs of Meeting the Interim Goals of the 1972 Act for Municipal Waste Treatment, 1972–81
Billions of current dollars

Type of treatment	Amount
Waste treatment facilities and collector systems	
Cumulative costs, 1972–81	77
Annual costs in 1981	10
Treatment of urban storm runoff	
Cumulative costs, 1972–81	120
Annual costs in 1981	11

Sources: Data for waste treatment facilities and collector systems are based on *Environmental Quality: The Fourth Annual Report of the Council on Environmental Quality* (1973), Table 5, p. 93. Urban runoff estimates for 1972–81 are based on *Water Policies for the Future*, Final Report to the President and to the Congress of the United States by the National Water Commission (1973), Table 16-13, p. 514. The NWC estimates give cumulative costs for the 1972–83 period and annual costs in 1983. The estimates above for 1972–81 and the annual costs in 1981 represent rough adjustments of NWC figures by the authors.

ticable" standards for water pollution control and the air quality standards under the 1970 amendments. These estimates, summarized in Table 6-2, exclude the automotive industry, which is discussed next.

The National Water Commission made a stab at estimating the costs to industry of achieving the 1983 goal of "best available technology."[4] For the twelve-year period 1972–83, they put the total cost at $116 billion, which probably implies an average cost in the early 1980s of $12 billion to $13 billion per year (compared with the $6 billion for achieving "best practicable treatment" shown in Table 6-2).

Automotive Industry Costs

The stringent standards for auto emissions set by the 1970 air quality legislation, if implemented, will give rise to several different kinds of costs. Automobiles will cost more because of the emission control equipment; consumers will incur higher operating and maintenance expenditures, since the devices now being developed by the auto companies will reduce gasoline mileage if the tightest standards are met, and will require periodic maintenance; and state governments will have to spend substantial sums to operate inspection

4. *Water Policies for the Future,* Final Report to the President and to the Congress of the United States by the National Water Commission (1973), p. 75.

Table 6-2. Costs to Industry of Meeting Air and Interim Water Quality
Standards, 1972–81ᵃ

Billions of current dollars

Environment	Cumulative costs, 1972–81	Costs in 1981
Air	38	6
Water	44	6
Total	82	12

Source: Based on data in *Environmental Quality: The Fourth Annual Report of the Council on Environmental Quality*, p. 93.
a. Excludes automotive industry.

services, since emission control will probably deteriorate over the life of a car.[5]

The 1973 Report of the Council on Environmental Quality estimated that the approach to emission control currently being followed by the automobile manufacturers would cost $59 billion between 1972 and 1981, including $10.5 billion in the latter year. The National Academy of Sciences reported figures in early 1973 that implied that the typical automobile (an eight-cylinder, standard model) would probably cost $370 more than those meeting 1970 standards, and that annual operating and maintenance costs would rise $200. By the time that all 100 million automobiles on the road are equipped with the new devices, the cost of controlling emissions will be $23.5 billion per year.

Other Major Costs

In addition to the three major elements discussed above, meeting the goals of the 1970 and 1972 acts would impose other kinds of costs.

As the previous chapter pointed out, even with stringent controls on automotive emissions, many major American cities will not be

5. As we pointed out in a previous chapter, the 1970 air quality legislation requires a 90 percent reduction in HC, CO, and NO_X, the first two to be achieved by 1975 and the last by 1976. The EPA administrator was allowed to postpone the dates for one year, and he has done so. Legislation pending at the time of this writing extends the final deadline for 90 percent reduction yet another year, to 1977 for HC and CO and to 1978 for NO_X. In addition, the legislation allows for a further suspension of all three standards for one more year if the auto makers prove that they need it.

Table 6-3. Capital Cost of Water Pollution Control, by Selected Nonpoint
Pollutant Source

Billions of dollars

Pollutant source	Pre-1972 standards	"No-discharge" policy
Acid mine drainage	5–15	10–30
Agricultural runoff	1–7	2–14
Oil and hazardous spills	1–5	2–10
Dredging spoil disposal and miscellaneous	1–2	2–4
Total	8–29	16–58

Source: *Water Policies for the Future*, Final Report, National Water Commission, Table 16-14, p. 516.

able, in the late 1970s, to meet standards for ambient air quality without imposing major restrictions on travel. Los Angeles would be subject to drastic curbs; and many other cities would have to cut back auto travel substantially.

In the case of water, the large nonpoint sources of pollutants pose major and costly problems for control. Agricultural wastes are heavy offenders, principally via the runoff from feedlots and large poultry farms. Coal mines are a source of acid drainage; oil spills and disposal of dredging spoil raise other problems. Again, there is little basis for firm estimates of the costs of dealing with these problems, principally because there is no agreement on the most appropriate technical solutions. The estimates in Table 6-3 were made by the National Water Commission; in each case they cover a very wide range.[6]

Total Costs

It is virtually impossible to sum the various estimates to arrive at a firm total for the national costs of reaching the goals set forth in the 1970 and 1972 legislation. Some of the legislative requirements have not yet been translated into specific regulations. A number of standards have recently been relaxed and postponed, principally in response to the energy situation. And even where specific targets for pollutant discharges have been issued and remain in

6. These problems of nonpoint sources, and the costs of alleviating them, are even less well delineated than those of point sources, for which at least tentative estimates have been made.

force, information about the cost of meeting them is far from complete. Hence, only a gross judgment can be made about overall national costs.

Early in this chapter a summary estimate of approximately $375 billion was given as the cost between now and 1983 of meeting the targets of the 1970 air pollution legislation and the interim standards of the 1972 water quality legislation. Since those estimates were made some standards have been relaxed or postponed. And the estimates themselves appear to assume principally "end-of-the-pipe" treatment of water pollutants, a high-cost way of dealing with the problem. But these reasons for believing that the estimates may be overstated are far more than offset by the fact that they exclude a number of very large costs, principally those of dealing with nonpoint sources of water pollution, and of meeting the air quality standards under conditions in which the price of gasoline and low-sulfur fuels has increased dramatically. Taking all of these factors into account, it is not unreasonable to set a conservative estimate of $500 billion as the overall national cost of meeting, by the early 1980s, the goals set forth in the 1970 and 1972 legislation (ignoring, in the latter case, the ultimate zero-discharge goal). In turn this implies an annual national outlay of $60 billion for air and water pollution control in the later years of the period.

The pollution control expenditures of federal, state, and local governments must come either from higher taxes or from curtailment of other governmental programs. We have seen how consumers will bear the very large outlays for auto emission control. The public utility, pulp and paper, food processing, chemical, and primary metal industries will be particularly affected by controls, whereas light industries that deposit few residuals in the environment will face few charges.

If costs of pollution control increase to $50 billion or $60 billion per year by the early 1980s, they will absorb about 10 percent of the growth in per capita national income which would otherwise be available to raise living standards and improve conditions in other ways. (If the zero-discharge goal is taken seriously, the fraction would be substantially greater.) On the one hand this is a large cost. It reflects a giant shift in national priorities reaching dramatically beyond that Senator Muskie voiced concern about in 1971. Its magnitude underlines the importance of weighing carefully the benefits and costs of increasing the stringency of controls, and of designing control programs so as to minimize the costs of achieving any given objective.

On the other hand, these huge numbers should not scare the nation into the folly of attempting to control pollution by halting economic growth. Even if we assume that ameliorating other forms of environmental damage (noise, radiation, solid waste, and so on) will cost as much as controlling air and water pollution, the total amounts involved would absorb less than one-quarter of the growth in per capita national income. The rest would still be available for other purposes. Halting growth just to stop environmental damage would be equivalent to throwing the other part away.[7] Moreover, bringing economic growth to a stop would not *reduce* the present degree of pollution—it would simply freeze it or slow the increase. Hence, arresting growth would not only be an incredibly wasteful means of pollution control, it would also fail badly in achieving the objectives in the 1970 and 1972 acts, which call for an absolute reduction in pollution levels.

Factors Affecting Costs

The costs of pollution control estimated in the prior sections are not engraved on stone. Three kinds of decisions can alter them: first, the stringency of the goals set for control policy; second, the speed of attempts to meet those goals; and third, the efficiency of the control programs.

Stringency of Goals

As chapters 3 and 4 pointed out, the failure of control policy and the deterioration of air and water in the 1960s prompted the Congress, in the 1970 amendments to the Clean Air Act and the 1972 amendments to the Water Pollution Control Act, not only to adopt new control mechanisms but also to set much more ambitious goals, specified at the national level. In the case of water pollution the new law set forth an ultimate goal of zero discharge.

---

7. Other arguments for slowing economic growth could be made—a desire for more leisure, for resource conservation, for a quieter, more settled life-style, and so on. Our point here is that stopping growth to prevent pollution would be simply foolish.

Table 6-4. Municipal and Industrial Costs at Various Levels of Water
Pollution Removal, 1971–81[a]

Kind of treatment		Cost of treatment (billions of dollars)		
Percentage of wastes treated	Percentage removal	Municipal waste treatment	Industrial control	Total
100	100	141.8	174.7	316.5
20	100	} 72.4	84.9	157.3
80	95–99			
100	95–99	54.9	63.9	118.8
100	85–90[b]	26.8	34.0	60.8

Source: U.S. Environmental Protection Agency, *The Economics of Clean Water* (1972), Vol. 1, Tables
2 and 3, pp. 153 and 154.
a. Includes both capital and operating costs, but excludes costs of dealing with urban storm runoff.
b. This is roughly the pre-1972 "uniform secondary treatment" standard.

Several years ago EPA estimated the overall costs of achieving
various levels of pollution removal for waterborne wastes (see
Table 6-4). Removing 85 to 90 percent of the pollutants from all
industrial and municipal effluents would cost $61 billion over the
1971–81 decade. Increasing removal to the range of 95 to 99 percent for all effluent would raise costs to $119 billion. Going a step
further, and removing 100 percent of the pollutants from one-fifth
of the wastes, while continuing to provide 95 to 99 percent removal
for the remainder, would require an additional $38 billion, bring-
ing the total to $157 billion. Finally, removing the last few per-
centage points from all wastes—a zero-discharge policy—would
approximately double these costs, for a total of $317 billion.

Even with these vast sums, the achievement of a zero-discharge
goal is technically doubtful; moreover, these sums take into account
neither the outlays to handle urban runoff and agricultural and
mine wastes nor the effects on other environmental media when
waterborne wastes are converted to solids or gases. Achieving zero
discharge in all media simultaneously is strictly impossible. The fact
that costs escalate very rapidly as the removal goals are raised even
modestly does not itself argue for choosing unambitious goals. But
the magnitude of these incremental costs clearly lays an obligation
on decision makers to scrutinize the benefits and costs of proposed
increases in goals. As chapter 4 pointed out, however, except for
those that appear in the federal budget, costs played little part in
the legislative deliberations on the 1970 and 1972 acts.

The Effect of Speed

Environmental goals can be achieved at widely different costs, depending on how rapidly they are met. The impact of timing on pollution control costs is well illustrated by the pace of construction of municipal waste treatment plants. According to a recent EPA survey[8] some $60 billion (measured in 1973 prices) will have to be invested by municipalities in the fiscal years 1974–77 to meet the requirements for water pollution control laid down in the 1972 act and other federal or state regulations. Some $37 billion of this amount will be needed to construct waste treatment plants and interceptor sewers, principally to meet the law's mandate that all municipalities provide secondary treatment of wastes by July 1, 1977. Corrective work on sewer systems will absorb most of the remaining $23 billion.

Table 6-5 compares the $37 billion of waste treatment and related construction requirements with recent trends in this type of construction. Between 1965 and 1971 the *real* value of such con-

Table 6-5. Federally Assisted Construction Starts for Waste Treatment Plants, Calendar Years 1965–71, and "Needs" Survey for Fiscal Years 1974–77

Calendar year	Value of starts (millions of current dollars)	Percentage change from prior year		
		Value of starts	Construction prices	Real value of construction
1965	365	...	...	...
1966	490	34.1	3.9	30.2
1967	397	−18.9	2.9	−21.8
1968	671	69.0	2.8	66.2
1969	937	39.6	7.3	32.3
1970	1,361	45.2	7.8	37.4
1971	1,700	24.9	15.0	9.9

EPA "Needs" Survey	Annual average	Four-year total
Value of construction		
Millions of 1971 dollars	7,700	30,800
Millions of 1973 dollars	9,150	36,600

Sources: 1965–71 data: *Economics of Clean Water*, Vol. 1, Table 12, p. 136. 1974–77 "needs": U.S. Environmental Protection Agency, "Costs of Construction of Publicly-Owned Wastewater Treatment Works: 1973 'Needs' Survey" (1973; processed), p. B-1. The translation of construction needs expressed in 1973 dollars into 1971 dollars was based on the 1971–73 construction cost increase cited on p. B-2 of the EPA Needs Survey. The percentages in the second column are calculated from data before rounding.

8. U.S. Environmental Protection Agency, "Costs of Construction of Publicly-Owned Wastewater Treatment Works: 1973 'Needs' Survey" (1973; processed).

struction rose at an average rate of 26 percent per year. In the latter part of the period, construction costs jumped sharply, in part at least because of the rapid growth in demand. In order to meet the targets of the 1972 act, real construction outlays would have to grow at an average annual rate of 40 percent for six years, almost double the rate of growth achieved in the earlier period. On the basis of past experience the attempt to crowd this much construction into a short span of time will very likely cause a significant part of federal grants and state and local funds to be dissipated in sharp price increases.

Other things being equal, it is clearly desirable to achieve environmental goals sooner than later. But construction schedules that overtax the capacity of the industry to expand, and the lack of a mechanism to enforce effective operation of completed plants, may well spur a rapid rise in costs, create a series of poorly run and underutilized facilities, and thus, perversely, delay solutions of pollution problems.

The relationship between costs and environmental deadlines is clearly revealed by automotive emission controls. The very tight deadlines for meeting the stringent requirements imposed by the 1970 act on automobile manufacturers virtually guarantee retention of the basic internal combustion engine with its expensive, complex, and hard-to-maintain control devices. As an earlier section of this chapter noted, this approach may add, according to some estimates, as much as $23.5 billion a year to the nation's annual bill for automotive transportation. In the short time allowed to meet the requirements, the manufacturers can hardly undertake the research, experimentation, and retooling to replace the internal combustion engine with a more radical, but less expensive and more reliable alternative. And once they have decided to modify the internal combustion engine, and have equipped it with control devices, their very heavy investments will foreclose, for quite a while, any shift toward a more radical solution. Chapter 7 discusses this problem in some detail, and offers alternative suggestions for a system of regulation and taxes designed to encourage a less costly and more reliable answer to automotive emission problems. The central point here is that the shortness of the deadlines established in the law may itself swell the ultimate cost of achieving the prescribed quality.

The Efficiency of Pollution Control Programs

Controls on air and water pollution impinge on an incredibly complex situation. The facts that determine how much pollution industries, cities, and transportation systems cause vary from firm to firm, location to location, and season to season. So do the costs of pollution reduction, depending on the circumstances facing a polluter. As a consequence, the effectiveness and the costs of alternative policies for pollution control can differ sharply, in accordance with their suitability to deal with this diversity.

A simple example highlights the efficiency of effluent or emission charges in contrast to a regulation specifying uniform reduction. If an effluent charge of, say, 10¢ a pound for BOD were levied, each firm would weigh the charges against the cost of waste reduction in an effort to minimize its total discharge costs. Since the costs of removing an additional unit of waste tend to rise with the percentage removed, it would pay the firm to push to the point where its incremental costs of removal equaled the effluent charge. Below that point, waste reduction would be less costly than the effluent charge; above it, the effluent charge would be cheaper. The lower the incremental costs of waste reduction, therefore, the higher the optimum removal percentage. A uniform effluent charge along a river basin would thus tend to produce a pattern of responses that concentrated pollution reduction where the costs were least. Regulations specifying a uniform percentage reduction of pollutants by all firms, on the other hand, ignore differences in costs and consequently yield a much more expensive solution.

A number of studies illustrate the wide range of costs associated with different approaches to pollution control. A combined hydrological, engineering, and economic analysis of the Delaware River Basin concluded that, for achieving any given level of water quality, an incentives strategy, relying on effluent charges, that concentrated discharge reduction where it was cheapest would cost 40 to 50 percent less than uniform treatment requirements.[9] A similar gap ap-

9. This study is summarized in Allen V. Kneese and Blair T. Bower, *Managing Water Quality: Economics, Technology, Institutions* (Johns Hopkins Press for Resources for the Future, 1968). A relatively simple solution, which imposes a single effluent charge on BOD throughout the basin, ensures the 40 to 50 percent

pears in the costs of the two methods for achieving 85 to 90 percent reduction of BOD among industries in the Great Lakes region.[10] An analysis of the cost of reducing sulfur emissions, which compared the costs of uniform regulation with those of emission charges, found that the latter strategy offered costs savings of over 35 to 40 percent.[11]

Since merely approaching the objectives of present legislation involves at the very least half a trillion dollars over the next fifteen years, the efficient design of programs for pollution abatement is critically important to the living standards of every American.

Harnessing Technological Progress

Any attempt to specify the costs of reducing air and water pollution is handicapped by the need to make some assumptions about technology. One of the characteristics that distinguish modern industrial society from its predecessors is its ability to develop new technologies in response to particular needs. Whenever a resource was treated as a free or renewable good with no penalties on its depletion, as the environment was until recently, technological advance promoted its consumption rather than its conservation. But technology can be an ingenious servant of conservation when society rewards it. For only one example, technology and capital investment have succeeded in halving labor requirements per unit of output every twenty-five to thirty years. Over the long haul, perhaps the most important single criterion on which to judge environmental policies is the extent to which they spur new technology toward the efficient conservation of environmental quality.

Judged in this light, many of our pollution control policies are sorely wanting. Auto emission controls pay no attention to the potentialities of new engine developments. The law that stipulates water effluent limits based on the "best available technology eco-

---

cost reduction. Even larger savings would accrue from more complex schemes of effluent charges.

10. Ivars Gutmanis, "The Generation and Cost of Controlling Air, Water, and Solid Waste Pollution: 1970–2000," an analysis prepared for the Brookings Institution (April 1972; processed).

11. EPA, Office of Research and Development, Memorandum on Sulfur Oxide Tax, March 15, 1974.

nomically achievable" discourages innovation because that would put firms in the ironic position of handing the regulatory authorities the means of imposing on them new and more costly standards of pollution control.

No matter how suitable the best technology available in 1985 may be for dealing with the problems in 1985, it will not be adequate to do the environmental job in 2000 or 2025. Unless we want to blight the fruits of economic growth, we shall have to be continuously pressing on the technological frontier in the search for means of accommodating economic progress within a clean environment. Anything that tends to freeze the technology of pollution control and to remove the incentive for technological advance will not only raise the costs of control, but beget ever-deteriorating environmental standards.

In one sense technology has helped create pollution. A society with no chemicals, automobiles, blast furnaces, or electric utilities would have fewer sources of air and water pollution.[12] The problem lies not with technological progress itself, however, but with the specific form it has taken. Ultimately, achieving a cleaner environment at reasonable costs will hinge critically on adaptation of the institutions of society to encourage the imaginative use of technology for the conservation of environmental assets.

Conclusions

The fact that the nation's commitment to environmental cleanup will impose massive costs is in itself no reason to retrench on the commitment. But their very size does make costs a central factor in the design of control policy. The difference between inefficient and efficient control policies can mean scores, perhaps hundreds, of billions of dollars released for other useful purposes over the next several decades. More careful consideration of the speed with which environmental goals are pursued can also make a substantial difference in costs, and, especially in the case of automotive exhaust emissions, could ensure effective solution to the long-run problem.

---

12. On the other hand, pre-industrial societies had pollution problems of their own—open municipal sewers, disease-breeding water supplies, and filthy rivers, to mention but a few.

An awareness of the way in which costs escalate as environmental goals are pushed toward a zero-discharge target would permit a better ordering of national priorities.

Most of the costs of pollution control do not show up in the federal budget. They never appear on any single accounting record. While this fact does not make them any less real, it has hidden them away from the scrutiny of legislative policy makers. To be aware of costs is not to be in favor of the status quo. Indeed, more awareness of costs in framing the legislation of recent years might have given the nation more effective, as well as less costly, control policies.

CHAPTER SEVEN

Alternative Strategies

SO FAR, this book has been a rather long, but we hope not tedious, account of the failures and continuing problems of federal environmental policy in the United States. In this chapter we examine alternative strategies based explicitly upon the recognition that, at their core, pollution problems result from the failure of the market system to generate the proper incentives for the allocation and management of a particular type of resources—those with common-property characteristics. We begin with water and air pollution and then consider the failure of incentives in environmental management in general.

A Decade of Research

To understand the importance of some ten years of accumulated research on the economics of water quality management, one must recognize that sanitary engineers (until recently the only profession giving any real attention to pollution) and public policy makers in the United States have seen the problem almost entirely in terms of the treatment of municipal and industrial wastewaters. Historically, they have given scant attention to technologies other than treatment plants and have utterly ignored the economic incentives bearing on the generation and discharge of residual materials.

About a decade ago, an economic paradigm was proposed for research in the area of water quality.[1] This was the concept of a hypothetical "basin-wide firm." The river basin or other watercourse was viewed as an asset that could produce many services—high-quality water for drinking, recreation, and wildlife; stream flow

1. Allen V. Kneese, *Water Pollution: Economic Aspects and Research Needs* (Resources for the Future, 1962).

85

for navigation; and a sink for human and industrial wastes. Each of these uses has a value for society, but they compete with each other. Using the stream as a sink reduces its value for recreation; holding pollution to a minimum raises costs for the firms and municipalities along the river. If a single firm (or government) were charged with managing the asset for society's benefit, it would seek to allocate the uses and deal with the wastes so as to gain the greatest possible net value for society.

In designing an optimum management system to meet this goal, the basin-wide firm would have to depart from society's traditional ways of coping with water management problems. First, since polluting wastes lower the quality of the asset that the firm is charged with managing, it would have to treat such wastes as costs, just as real as any other costs of operation and just as important to minimize.

Second, in addition to treatment of wastewater, an optimum management system for the basin-wide firm would have to include such alternatives as regulation of stream flow; a variety of measures for the improvement of in-stream water quality; the diversion of wastewaters from sensitive areas; their use for irrigation; short-term, high-level treatment measures; and a revision of the incentive system bearing on the generation and disposal of wastewaters. None of these technological and policy options was, strictly speaking, new. Most of them had found application in isolated instances. But they had not generally been regarded as possibilities to be systematically and routinely considered along with waste treatment in water quality management and, of course, the market provided no incentive for their use.

Finally, an optimal management system would not impose a uniform reduction of wastes on each industrial activity, municipality, and other source. Rather, it would adjust the degree of pollution removal required of each activity so as to minimize the total cost of cleanup for the river basin as a whole.

Based on this framework, a series of case studies was launched to test the applicability of this approach to water quality management in real situations. They provide compelling evidence that a system of regional water quality management, using a wide range of technologies for improving water quality and employing economic incentives to encourage their adoption in the optimum combination, would be far superior in both cost and effectiveness to the present legalistic approach, which emphasizes treatment technology and a regulatory approach to effluent standards and enforcement.

The Evidence

Studies of the Potomac River Basin, the Delaware Estuary area, the San Francisco Bay, the Raritan Bay, the Miami River Basin in Ohio, and the Wisconsin River Basin, among others, leave hardly any doubt about the general validity of this conclusion.[2] Each of these studies analyzed alternative approaches to achieving a specified set of water quality standards. In every case, the best alternative included a combination of techniques ranging from the mechanical reaeration of river basins to the pumping of groundwater for low-flow augmentation. Compared to the conventional approach, which relies on uniform treatment of all wastes, the superior alternatives offered sharply lower costs. Moreover, as we remarked in chapter 2, such regional measures may be the only way of dealing with nonpoint sources of pollution such as agricultural runoff.

Even more important than the exploration and implementation of a wide range of technical options is the use of economic incentives as a device to achieve pollution control. Economic incentives, in the form of taxes or "effluent charges" levied on each unit of pollution discharged into the watercourse, have three advantages: First, the imposition of effluent charges encourages a pattern of waste management among different firms and municipalities that tends to minimize the costs of control for the river basin as a whole. Second, charges are much more likely to be enforceable than is the chief alternative, the setting of effluent limits on individual firms and municipalities by a regulatory agency. Third, charges provide a continuing incentive to adopt improved technology as it comes along.

Effluent Charges and Cost Minimization

The overall costs of control are minimized by concentrating the reduction in pollution most heavily among those firms and activities

---

2. The reader can find a reasonably current review of the results of the pertinent research, including most of the cases mentioned in this section, in Allen V. Kneese and Blair T. Bower, *Managing Water Quality: Economics, Technology, Institutions* (Johns Hopkins Press for Resources for the Future, 1968).

whose costs of reduction are least.[3] An efficient approach to pollution control, therefore, requires that different firms reduce pollution by differing amounts, depending on the costs of reduction. Moreover, besides applying conventional waste treatment, each firm should take advantage of a wide range of control alternatives—modifying its production processes, recycling its by-product wastes, and using raw materials and producing varieties of its product that cause less pollution.

In theory, a regulatory agency could devise an efficient plan for uniform reduction of pollution. Effluent limitations for each type of polluting activity could be designed to achieve the minimum-cost solution. In practice, however, the need to tailor limits to each firm, and to consider for each the cost and effectiveness of all of the available alternatives for reducing pollution, would be an impossible task. There are up to 55,000 major sources of industrial water pollution alone. A regulatory agency cannot know the costs, the technological opportunities, the alternative raw materials, and the kinds of products available for every firm in every industry. Even if it could determine the appropriate reduction standards for each firm, it would have to revise them frequently to accommodate changing costs and markets, new technologies, and economic growth.

Effluent charges, on the other hand, tend to elicit the proper responses even in the absence of an omniscient regulatory agency. Each source of pollution would be required to pay a tax on every unit of pollutant it discharged into the air or water. Faced with these effluent charges, a firm would pursue its own interest by reducing pollution by an amount related to the cost of reduction.

An example of pollution removal costs for a hypothetical firm helps make the point:

Percentage of BOD removed	Cost of removing an additional pound of BOD (cents)
40	2
60	4
80	7
90	10
95	15
99	40

3. This is an oversimplification. The impact on water quality from the wastes of any firm depends on the firm's location along the river basin and the hydrology

In these circumstances, if an effluent charge of 10 cents were imposed on each pound of biological oxygen demand (BOD) discharged, the firm would find it profitable to remove 90 percent of the BOD from its effluent because the cost of removal is less than the effluent charge up to that point. The firm would choose to discharge the remaining 10 percent of BOD, however, since the cost of removing it would be greater than the effluent charge. If the charge were raised to 15 cents, the firm would now find it profitable to remove 95 percent of the BOD. In other words, an effluent charge can be set high enough to accomplish any desired degree of pollution removal.

Each firm would be faced with different removal costs, depending on the nature of its production process and its economic situation. For any given effluent charge, firms with low costs of control would remove a larger percentage than would firms with high costs —precisely the situation needed to achieve a least-cost approach to reducing pollution for the economy as a whole. Firms would tend to choose the least expensive methods of control, whether treatment of wastes, modification in production processes, or substitution of raw materials that had less serious polluting consequences. Further, the kinds of products whose manufacture entailed a lot of pollution would become more expensive and would carry higher prices than those that generated less, so consumers would be induced to buy more of the latter.

The effluent-charge approach has another characteristic that recommends it over the regulatory approach. A firm has no incentive to cut pollution further once it has achieved the effluent limitation specified by regulation. Indeed, it has a positive incentive *not* to do so, since the additional reduction is costly and lowers profits. Because effluent charges must be paid for every unit of pollution firms have not removed, they would have a continuing incentive to de-

---

of the stream. A least-cost solution for achieving any given level of ambient water quality would, therefore, have to take into account both the firm's location and the stream's hydrology. Each firm's effluent would have to be weighted by its impact on water quality along particular reaches of the watercourse. In a least-cost solution, each firm would then have to cut back its effluent to the point where its marginal cost per *weighted* unit of effluent reduction was the same as that for every other firm. But the Delaware study, reviewed below, shows that a fairly simple system of effluent charges could come close, in terms of costs, to the more complicated least-cost solution for the whole system.

vote research and engineering talent to finding less costly ways of achieving still further reductions. This continuing incentive is important. The quantity of air and water available to the nation is fixed, roughly speaking. But as economic activity grows over time, the volume of pollution discharged into the air and water will rise unless an ever-increasing percentage of pollutants is removed.

Economists have long advocated, in abstract terms, a tax or charge on activities like pollution that impose costs on society but are not recognized in the accounting that underlies business decisions. Such a tax would automatically force each decision maker to reckon the social costs of his activities. This approach was foreign to the engineering profession, however, and to those most responsible for public policy in this area; and, until quite recently, they have usually greeted it with skepticism when they became aware of it. Even some of those—including some economists—who acknowledge its theoretical merit have been dubious of its practicability. Others have felt that it would elicit little response from polluters, who would simply pass the cost on to consumers and proceed as before.

Economic research has tended to support the practical value and effectiveness of an effluent-charge or tax approach. In the most pertinent case study, it was found that effluent charges could achieve a given water quality objective in the Delaware Estuary area at about half the cost of a regulatory approach aimed at uniform reductions. The efficacy of charges is also supported by the response of industrial firms when they become subject to municipal sewer surcharges, geared to the amount of pollution content of wastewaters. Even though such charges were much lower than a true effluent charge would be, the amount of wastes discharged to the municipal sewer system usually fell dramatically.

Finally, the effectiveness and efficiency of a regional approach to water quality management are supported by study of the successful programs developed over seventy years by agencies in the Ruhr area of West Germany (which includes several river basins other than the Ruhr). These agencies were granted broad authority; and the principles of water quality laid down for them in their basic charter included a broad range of technological options which they systematically combined according to economic criteria. As a result, they have evolved an approach, and a set of policies and facilities, in which economic incentives play an important role. In general they resemble those that a hypothetical basin-wide firm might adopt when charged with maximizing the net value to society of the services provided by the basin.

Enforceability: Regulation versus Effluent Charges

Governmental folklore has it that regulation and enforcement are direct, effective, and dead-sure means for attacking market failures. Studies of how the regulatory process has worked in general, coupled with our review in chapter 5 of its operation with respect to pollution problems, reveal that it is instead cumbersome, corruptible, and arbitrary and capricious in its impact.

The regulatory approach suffers from an inescapable dilemma. If the system is simple enough to be handled by a central bureaucracy, as one might have thought was true for the uniform treatment strategy in effect before 1972, it is bound to be very inefficient. But if it seeks to accommodate the tremendous diversity of the economy, and tries to devise effluent standards that minimize costs, the regulatory task becomes insurmountable. The resulting—and unavoidable—arbitrariness and inequity will in turn make the enforcement of regulatory limits in the courts difficult, time-consuming, and ultimately ineffective. Furthermore, even if the program were successfully administered, dischargers would undoubtedly view the greatly differing limits they faced as highly inequitable.

Law makers have exhibited skepticism about the effectiveness of market-like devices such as effluent taxation. But what we know about the impacts of price changes, and the limited evidence specifically about effluent taxes, provides strong arguments for their superiority over regulation. They constitute a relatively neutral device whose enforcement could be incorporated into the body of precedent and experience already surrounding the nation's tax laws. The imposition of charges or taxes would require that effluents be metered at each outfall. But regulations also call for metering. From that point on, the payment and collection of effluent taxes involve no major administrative burdens; and, more important, they raise no specter of court battles over case-by-case regulatory decisions. While there is much tax litigation, the great bulk of taxes— especially excise taxes, which most resemble effluent charges—are paid without legal struggles.

Effluent charges have another strong advantage over regulation, especially important in times like the present, when much of the national program of air pollution control seems to be falling victim to the energy crisis. That advantage is that the responses they call for can be flexible, but they always call for some sort of response. When "tough" restrictions are relaxed or eliminated, the continuing social costs of the pollutant discharges are in no way reflected in the discharger's decision making. He is "home free" so to speak. Furthermore, whatever effectiveness the enforcement approach may have is entirely dependent on constant, vigorous enforcement, which can easily give way before the shifting enthusiasms, fears, and perceptions of problems by the public and its representatives. In a government that proceeds from crisis to crisis, as ours often does, this is an extremely important problem for the enforcement approach.

Other Advantages of an Effluent-Charge Strategy

To the extent that the subsidy-regulatory system is effective in reducing discharge, it tends to bias choice toward the less efficient control techniques. Only treatment plants qualify for subsidies; and treatment processes are likely to be emphasized because they are easy to identify and to specify in regulations based on the status of technology. Such is the strategy in the 1972 water quality legislation. This strategy promotes the construction of waste treatment facilities by industry, although in many, if not most, cases other approaches would be cheaper. Effluent charges, on the other hand, are neutral: they do not favor waste treatment or any other single technique, but induce firms to reduce pollution by the most economical means.

The 1972 water quality legislation does reduce the bias toward waste treatment embodied in earlier policy. Previously, industrial firms whose wastes were processed by municipalities had an advantage from the heavy subsidization of the treatment plants by federal construction grants. Even if the municipalities charged firms enough to cover municipal costs, the fees were still lower than full economic costs. The 1972 amendments required industrial firms to pay a fee reflecting their appropriate share of the full costs of the municipal plant. But the provisions of the tax code that allow firms an accelerated writeoff of waste treatment facilities remain in force, and provide a biased subsidy for one form of pollution control. Furthermore, tax-exempt bond financing for industrial pollution abatement facilities has expanded rapidly. In 1973 such financing rose to nearly $1.8 billion, from zero in 1971. A recent survey indicates that, exclusive of tax-exempt bank loans, which are unreported, it could total $2.9 billion in 1974, or about 40 percent of industry's own reported plans for spending on air and water pollution control during the year.[4] This subsidy (since it is for separate pollution control facilities) has the same technological bias as tax writeoffs and grants.

An additional advantage of effluent charges lies in the fact that they yield revenue rather than straining an already seriously over-extended tax system. This revenue can be put to useful public purposes, including improvements in the quality of our environment. From the point of view of fiscal policy, the ideal tax base is an activity that generates social costs. Taxes on such activities not only yield revenue but, if properly designed, improve the allocation of resources by moving private costs closer to social costs. This is important because most conventional taxes tend to distort resource use in one way or another.

Industry has been emphasized so far in this discussion of charges, but municipalities too are paying only part of the social costs associated with the wastewaters they generate, and what they pay is capriciously distributed depending on how much treatment they have implemented and whether they waited for federal subsidies. Effluent charges would give these municipalities reasons to proceed expeditiously with the effective treatment of waste, which would reduce the charges they have to pay. Moreover, this system focuses on what is put in the stream and thereby offers an incentive for effective operations of existing facilities—a matter of great importance, as we saw in chapter 3. Finally, about half the residuals treated in municipal plants come from industrial sources. Thus, a charge on municipal discharges, passed back to these industrial sources, is necessary to motivate firms to curb generation of residuals.

4. See John J. Winders, "Tax-Exempt Anti-Pollution IRBs Level Off in Volume in 1st Half," *The Money Manager,* Vol. 3 (July 15, 1974), p. 48. A good discussion of such financing is found in Edward F. Renshaw, "Should the Federal Government Subsidize Industrial Pollution Control Investments?" *Journal of Environmental Economics and Management,* Vol. 1 (May 1974), pp. 84–88.

Some Equity Aspects

Public policy should be effective and efficient, but it should also meet our society's criteria of equity. Unfortunately, these criteria are not well defined. But they seem to say that we want to avoid worsening the distribution of personal income and to avoid imposing costs and requirements on some persons and industries that others similarly situated escape.

In general, by far the best way to meet equity criteria for personal income is to redistribute income directly, and a considerable amount (if, in our view, not enough) of this is done by progressive taxation and payments to poor people. A particularly bad way would be to let social costs like pollution go unpaid in order to keep prices down. Effluent charges, together with the internal controls they induce, bring private costs more in line with social costs; but whether the effect on prices would be greater or less than that of an enforcement program alone is unclear. The greater efficiency of the charges scheme could well wipe out any tendency for charges plus control costs to outweigh control costs alone under an enforcement scheme. In the Delaware case the two amounts were about the same, but the scheme of charges required only about half the cost in real resources—the remainder being revenue available for other governmental purposes.

Viewed by the waste dischargers themselves, effluent charges have desirable equity features. First, the sort of scheme we envisage would affect all waste dischargers at the same time, avoiding the erratic distribution of effects created by the permit-issuing–enforcement–appeals process. Second, the combination of charges paid and internal control costs incurred tends to be more evenly distributed among dischargers than the costs associated either with uniform cutbacks or with the minimum-cost strategy imposed through direct regulation.

While there are strong economic reasons for applying an effluent charge system to municipal waste discharges, formidable political objections would be raised against any proposals under which the federal government or regional water management bodies imposed taxes on "financially hard-pressed" local governments. To reduce these obstacles, the effluent charges paid by municipalities might be channeled into a special fund, to be redistributed to local governments (perhaps in inverse relation to their per capita pollution levels). They would then have substantial incentives to manage their wastes properly.

How to Institute Effluent Charges

Despite the apparently compelling reasons for favoring a system of effluent charges as one of the cornerstones of effective and efficient national and regional water quality management, it would be difficult for particular states and regions to pioneer such a marked departure from previous practice. Indeed, as we saw in the previous chapters, states may find it difficult or impossible to institute even the more conventional controls. Although several states and regions have taken initiatives recently, the federal government's greater insulation from powerful local interests gives it the opportunity for leadership.

There is much to recommend a national minimum charge that would establish the principle universally and blunt industry's threats to move to more permissive regions. Moreover, the charge could provide an immediate across-the-board incentive to reduce discharges into the nation's watercourses. Unlike the strategy embodied in the 1972 amendments, such a charge would affect every waste discharger immediately, unavoidably, and equitably. Had such a charge been levied at an adequately high level when it was first seriously proposed to the Congress in the sixties, there would surely have been a large improvement in water quality nearly everywhere rather than the deterioration that has actually occurred.

The national charge could be considered a minimum that, at their discretion, could be exceeded by state and regional agencies having responsibility for water quality management, according to their own objectives. Revenues obtained by the federal government could supplement funds from general tax sources and be made available for financing the federal program, with the excess turned over to other governments of general jurisdiction. As an illustrative calculation, if the charge for BOD were set at 15¢ per pound (a strong incentive to reduction, because it is well above the costs of higher-level treatment except at the smallest outfalls, and far above the cost of process changes in many industries), the annual revenues would be about $2 billion to $3 billion. On the assumption that charges for other substances would yield similar amounts, total annual revenues would be $4 billion to $6 billion.[5] But the amount would fall rapidly once the incentive took effect, probably to less than $1 billion after several years. Also it might be preferable to implement the charges in stages, increasing them annually until they reach full scale.

Regional Water Quality Management Agencies

The revenues from effluent charges could be used to help establish regional water quality management agencies, which are the other element in our proposed alternative strategy. One way for the federal government to encourage regional agencies would be to establish incentives and guidelines for their organization and operation, either under state law (where appropriate, these agencies could be the states themselves) or through interstate arrangements. An agency with adequate authority to plan and implement a regional system would be eligible for grants to pay staff and to make the first data collections, analyses, and formulation of specific measures for water quality management. Some of the money would also be made available for retraining some of the scientists and engineers now in surplus to do this work.

If the federal government is satisfied that the proposed regional program and the plan for its implementation meet criteria for effective and efficient operation, the agency might be eligible for a grant to assist it with actual construction and operating expenses. Such grants might appropriately be limited to the early implementation stage—say, five years. During this period, longer-term arrangements for financing the agency would have to be worked out, in which the revenues from the effluent charges could play a major role. Administration of the charges system would be turned over to the regional agencies with the federal level of charges as a baseline. In this manner, the same measures that financed the management of

5. BOD has been emphasized here because it is the single most common water-borne waste material and often a good indicator of other pollutants; but other substances should also be included in the charges scheme. Various weighting methods to establish equivalences have been suggested, but perhaps the best starting point would be the systems that have long been in effect in the Ruhr. See Kneese and Bower, *Managing Water Quality*.

the common-property asset on a regional scale would serve as incentives to waste dischargers to cut back on their emissions. Special provisions might be included in the federal law to protect marginal industrial plants in which there is a broad social interest; the adjustment provisions of our international trade law offer a pattern here. In these efforts, special attention should be given to assisting in the reemployment of labor, perhaps through retraining and subsidized movement. Assistance to the firms themselves is less desirable, because any plant that would shut down under the pressure of the program outlined here is probably in deep trouble anyway.

In emphasizing effluent charges, we do not mean to imply that administrative rulings and legal remedies are unimportant in water quality management. Indeed, the discharge of many substances (primarily heavy metals and persistent organics) should probably be prohibited entirely; Sax, among others, has suggested ways in which the courts could take a more constructive part in environmental management.[6] But we are persuaded that economic incentives and regional management are the central elements in effectively and efficiently coming to grips with the problem of water quality management, in the long term as well as the near term.[7]

Many of the elements of this alternative strategy were embodied in a bill introduced by Senator William Proxmire and a number of prominent cosponsors late in 1969; Congressman Lee H. Hamilton and others introduced identical legislation in the House.[8] These bills would have established a national effluent charge (unfortunately, for presumed reasons of political necessity, excluding municipalities) and provided incentives for the creation of regional agencies along the lines outlined above. As the reader will infer from the discussion in chapters 3 and 4, the bill was introduced at a time when strategic reconsideration of the approach embodied in earlier legislation should have been possible. Moreover, committees of the National Academy of Sciences, the Urban Coalition, and various consumer groups, among others, had gone on record supporting the incentives approach. Despite these facts and strong efforts by Senator Proxmire

6. Joseph L. Sax, *Defending the Environment: A Strategy for Citizen Action* (Knopf, 1971).
7. The engineering, legal, and political aspects of charges systems are explored in depth in a forthcoming Resources for the Future book.
8. S. 3181, November 1969; H.R. 12304, December 1971.

and others to get the Public Works Committee to take it seriously, the
approach was virtually ignored in the deliberations leading up to the
1972 amendments.[9]

As an interesting sidelight, however, we note that, over roughly
the same period, the major European countries were working out
strategies much more in keeping with the economic and technological realities of the problem. In some respects the most interesting case is West Germany, where a standards-permits-enforcement
strategy has been in effect since 1957. There is now a detailed proposal for a national effluent-charges law, a brief discussion of which
is presented in the appendix to this chapter. Approaches incorporating effluent charges and regional management have also been put
into effect or are being developed in France, Great Britain, Hol-
land, and Czechoslovakia.

Air Pollution Alternatives

Just like the formation of national policy, economic research in
the air pollution area, and policy proposals stemming from it,
lagged similar activity concerning water by several years. The central
ideas, methodology, and main results of the research were quite
similar in the two areas. The efficiency advantage of emission
charges, and of greater or lesser degrees of regional planning and
management, turned out to be, if anything, more spectacular for air
than for water. The first such study, in the Memphis metropolitan
area, compared the uniform-cutback approach with the cost-
minimizing systems that would be induced by emission charges, and
found the latter significantly less costly.[10] A later notable study, in
preparation for the President's proposal of what became the Air
Quality Act of 1967, involved construction of a composite model embodying elements from several major U.S. cities with severe problems

9. One can envisage a strategy that would incorporate the incentives-regional
approach and some of the better elements of the 1972 amendments. This could include strengthened planning and support for institution building, with emphasis
shifted to the regional scale; improved legal standing accorded interested parties;
control of toxic substances along the lines of the amendments; a permit program
for screening new industrial plants to ensure that their performance on residuals
generation matched that of, say, the top 25 percent of existing plants; and a
national program of stiff effluent fees.

10. See Azriel Teller, "Air-Pollution Abatement: Economic Rationality and
Reality," *Daedalus*, Vol. 96 (Fall 1967), pp. 1082–98.

associated with the discharge of sulfur oxides and particulates.[11] It was found that cost-minimizing programs could achieve the same environmental objectives at only 10 percent of the costs of the uniform-cutback method.[12] These results do not even include the more indirect efficiency effects, discussed in connection with water and equally valid here. Also equally valid are the equity and efficacy elements considered above.

Sulfur Oxides Tax

After further study by the Council on Environmental Quality, the Treasury Department, and the EPA, these considerations of efficiency, efficacy, and equity led President Nixon to propose the Pure Air Tax Act of 1972 in February 1972. The President had great difficulty in getting congressional attention for the resulting bill, but supported it again in his 1973 environmental message. A strong approach was especially needed in this area because of the severe health implications of sulfur oxides discharges.

To date, the switch from high- to low-sulfur fuels has been the primary reason for reduced emissions of sulfur oxides. As the events of late 1973 amply demonstrated, such a switch can readily be reversed—and its gains easily lost—especially if no economic penalties remain for emitting large quantities of sulfur oxides. The technologies for removing sulfur from fuels (especially coal) before burning, or from the exhaust streams, are on the drawing boards, but the past five years have seen little movement toward development of these alternatives. Here is a situation ripe for the application of a strategy based on economic incentives.

Levying a per-pound charge on the sulfur emitted by power plants and other industrial firms would elicit a variety of economic responses resulting in improved air quality.

1. The potential cost saving would lend a strong impetus to the development and installation of effective systems for sulfur removal.

11. See p. 17 above on the use of such models.
12. See Jack W. Carlson, "Discussion" of paper by Allen V. Kneese, "Environmental Pollution: Economics and Policy," both appearing in American Economic Association, *Papers and Proceedings of the Eighty-third Annual Meeting, 1970 (American Economic Review, Vol. 61, May 1971), pp. 153–66, 169–72. A fuller discussion is found in U.S. Department of Health, Education, and Welfare, Office of the Assistant Secretary (Planning and Evaluation), "An Economic Analysis of the Control of Sulphur Oxides Air Pollution" (HEW, 1967; processed).

2. Confronted with a charge on high-sulfur fuels, users of coal and oil with a range of fuel options would choose the low-sulfur fuels voluntarily, even though they are now more expensive.

3. By creating an economically based demand for low-sulfur fuels, the charge on sulfur oxide emissions would provide oil refiners with the strong incentive they now lack to remove sulfur in the refining process and to develop techniques for doing it less expensively. The sulfur content of coal can also be reduced by processing.

4. The emission charge would tend to divert consumers to commodities with less serious environmental effects by raising the prices of those whose production processes employ coal and oil for combustion.

The bill proposed by President Nixon would levy a tax, beginning with calendar year 1976, on emissions of sulfur to the atmosphere. The initial tax rate was calculated to induce curtailment in sulfur emissions sufficient to meet the 1975 air quality standards established by the Clean Air Amendments. In years after 1976, the tax rate would depend on a region's air quality in the preceding year; it would be 15¢ and 10¢ per pound, respectively, where primary and secondary standards were violated, and zero where all standards were met.

One problem with President Nixon's proposal is that it would encourage existing firms to move operations from "dirty" regions to "clean" regions, and new plants to settle there in the first place, to avoid paying a charge. Therefore, in time, shifts in industrial location would degrade the quality of air in the cleaner regions and bring the entire country down to the lowest common denominator.

This problem is at least partially dealt with in identical bills later proposed by Congressman Les Aspin (H.R. 10890) and Senator Proxmire (S. 3057), which would levy a flat national tax. Three main points of these bills are particularly worth noting. First, a target level of 20¢ per pound of sulfur would be reached in 5¢ increments from 1972 to 1975. The target is greater than the estimated costs of high-level abatement but less than the estimated average cost of damages across the nation (put by EPA at about 30¢ per pound). Second, the tax would be uniform across the nation, both to ensure administrative simplicity and to avoid creating havens for polluters.

Finally, because Congress, rather than an agency, would set the level of the tax, the debate would be out in the open.[13]

Automobiles

Even with today's relatively simple systems, maintenance of pollution control devices on automobiles is a very serious problem. Cars are tested before they are sold to see that they meet the emission standards already imposed on the manufacturer; but no follow-up assures that they continue to meet the standards, though a number of studies have shown that few can do so after as little as 10,000 to 15,000 miles of use. For example, results released by EPA in 1973 showed that over half of the vehicles tested after on-the-road service had higher emissions than the standards applicable to their model years.[14] Responding to the importance of maintenance and tuning, the 1970 law required manufacturers, starting with the 1975 models, to guarantee that their cars will continue to meet emission standards for 50,000 miles or five years—bringing on the technological and enforcement problems we have already reviewed.

How to solve the twin problems of ensuring maintenance and stimulating technology? Fifteen years ago economists at Rand Corporation proposed the answer—a smog tax.[15] In one, possibly very powerful, version of this tax, cars would be tested periodically and assigned a smog rating, indicated by a seal or coded device attached to the car. Then, when the driver purchased gasoline, he would pay a tax, over and above the basic gasoline taxes, that would vary with his smog rating.

An individual could reduce his smog tax bill in several ways.

1. Tuning up or overhauling his engine to reduce emissions and obtain better gas mileage would be an economical alternative to paying the tax. Recently established emission standards for cars regis-

13. As an interesting sidelight, two of three American Nobel Prize winners in economics joined many others in publicly favoring this proposal (the third did not comment). See Coalition to Tax Pollution, "The Sulfur Tax" (Washington: The Coalition, May 25, 1972; processed).

14. CALSPAN Corporation, *Automobile Exhaust Emission Surveillance: A Summary*, APTD-1544 (Research Triangle Park, N.C.: U.S. Environmental Protection Agency, Air Pollution Technical Information Center, 1973), pp. 4, 40.

15. D. M. Fort and others, "Proposal for a Smog Tax," reprinted in *Tax Recommendations of the President*, Hearings before the House Committee on Ways and Means, 91 Cong. 2 sess. (1970), pp. 369–79.

tered in New Jersey are less stringent for earlier than for more recent
model years. In a pilot study, 45 percent of the cars failed the state
standards. But more important, almost every car that failed could
pass after a regular "emission tune-up" by a trained mechanic at an
average cost of about $20.[16] The New Jersey work demonstrated
that vehicles can be efficiently tested (it takes about 35 seconds)
and that engine condition, including the recency and quality of
tune-up, is extremely important to emissions.

2. A car owner has many options that would allow him to drive
fewer miles per year—living closer to his job, using mass transit, or
participating in car pools. Standards based on emissions per vehicle-
mile do nothing whatsoever about miles driven, but the smog tax
would affect this extremely important variable, as well as emissions
per mile.

3. Control devices could be installed on older cars. In 1970, in
a market test, General Motors offered control kits for pre-1968
models at about $20 installed; but no one bought them. Clearly, it
was nonsensical to expect anyone to make this investment since,
without assurance that others would make it, any one person's effect
on the situation would be negligible. Similarly, no one would buy
the kit if he were sure that everyone else would so do: his air
would be equally clean whether he bought the kit or not—so why
bother? This is the "free rider" problem in the economic theory of
"public goods." A smog tax would introduce a new and persuasive
element into this calculation.

4. Because consumers would demand them, manufacturers
would have an incentive to design automobiles that had better smog
ratings not only when they rolled off the assembly line but throughout their lifetimes. In the long run this is probably the most important incentive effect of all.

Only the first of these four ways to reduce one's smog tax is
relevant to the question of who should be responsible for the continued attainment of emission standards. But the New Jersey study
suggests the practicability of placing the responsibility on owners
and backing it up with appropriate economic incentives. The tax
elicits other desirable responses from drivers, such as the last three

16. New Jersey Department of Environmental Protection, Bureau of Air Pollution Control, "Motor Vehicle Tune-up at Idle," The New Jersey REPAIR Project
(The Department, no date; processed).

alternatives, and its incentives apply to owners of pre-1968 cars that have no control systems, but whose emissions can often be cut substantially by better maintenance and certain retrofitted devices. The smog tax could be varied seasonally; and it could be raised in critical areas—for example, those with unworkable urban transit plans—as a powerful spur to car pooling, reduction in frivolous driving, use of available mass transit, and demand for more.

The gasoline surcharge is also adaptable to reflecting other external costs associated with the use of automobiles, such as highway and street congestion, and uncompensated social costs imposed by the manufacture of certain fuels. Size and fuel consumption variables could govern the amount of tax per gallon. The incentives to manufacturers to develop efficient low-emission technologies are obvious, and no deadline would act to freeze in a technology. For engine types that are inherently and dependably very low in emissions (such as Rankine engines), the smog tax might be canceled entirely.

We feel that a scheme of this type has many attractive features and should be tried. But, short of its full implementation, some of its incentives could be incorporated into the present law.

The Jacoby study recommends one way of doing this that would essentially extend the deadline and apply an economic incentive to innovation in the interim.[17] It would preserve the pre-1975 standards, and postpone the mandatory incorporation of the 1975–76 standards until 1981. A fine equivalent to 5 to 10 percent of its cost would be levied on a model that fell between interim standards and the full 1975–76 goals. In 1981 the full $10,000 fine would be levied on vehicles that did not meet the 1975–76 standards.

We would adapt the present law somewhat differently. The first element would be a slight reduction in the 1975 standard (now delayed) so that no catalytic converters would be needed to achieve it. Then we would institute a smog tax on automobiles progressively over the remainder of the decade until in 1981 the rate for a car still emitting at the 1974 new-car level would exceed the several hundred dollars per car associated with the catalytic system. A few urban areas with severe smog problems would be targeted for special treatment. We believe this strategy would almost certainly

17. Henry D. Jacoby, John D. Steinbruner, and others, *Clearing the Air: Federal Policy on Automotive Emissions Control* (Ballinger, 1973).

lead to the large-scale introduction of inherently low-emission and thermally efficient engines before the end of the decade.[18] It would clearly be second best since it would not influence behavior the way an emission tax levied on the motorist would; but it would be, we think, a vast improvement over the current system.

A Coherent Set of Fees for Atmospheric Emissions

Emission fees would have to be set on a number of different air pollutants. In calculating the appropriate fees, it would be important to set them in the proper relationship to each other, to prevent the adoption of processes that reduce one type of pollutant only to increase another. One such scheme is the "pindex" method of weighting according to toxicity; a sample fee has been calculated for California on this basis.[19] It starts with a fee calculated on the basis of an estimate of damage or control cost for a target level of removal and, on the basis of their relative toxicity, deduces the implied fee for other substances for which no direct measures of harmfulness have been calculated.

Concluding Comments on Effluent Fees

Enough work has been done on the use of effluent fees and regional management devices for water and air quality management to constitute a firm basis for a strategic alternative to the way we have been attacking these problems at the national level. While any practicable program will necessarily have many crudities and arbitrary elements, we feel that workable legislation based on this alternative not only is possible but also would be much more efficient, equitable, and effective—in both the short and the long run—than the legislation Congress has adopted. While the proposals we have reviewed share the difficulty of the present approach by treating closely related problems in isolation, they would mark a start toward the comprehensive and effective environmental management that we must ultimately achieve.

18. Such engines can almost certainly be developed. See, for example, Graham Walker, "The Stirling Engine," *Scientific American*, Vol. 229 (August 1973), pp. 80–87.
19. See A. M. Schneider, "An Effluent Fee Schedule for Air Pollutants Based on Pindex," *Journal of the Air Pollution Control Association*, Vol. 23 (June 1973), pp. 486–89.

Toward a Comprehensive Environmental Policy

The conservation of mass implies that the entire flow of materials and energy through the economy must show up as residuals to be returned to the various environmental media. Accordingly, efforts to reduce discharges into one medium will increase the burden on others unless the processes used permit the material to be recycled. For example, the sludge from wastewater treated in the usual plant is often incinerated, and a favorite way of removing particulates from stack gases is to scrub them with a stream of water. These considerations suggest simultaneously bringing all the various residuals under management in an integrated, coherent program. These relationships present tangled complexities for any approach to emissions control policy.

At the moment, economists and engineers are actively developing comprehensive models of residuals management that systematically embody all the major residuals from production and consumption activities.[20] Until such models become routinely applicable, and until appropriate regional institutions can be created to use them to formulate fully coherent management programs for all the media simultaneously, it is highly important that our national legislation at least recognize the basic nature of the problem.

A systematic attack on perverse incentives should proceed on two fronts. First, we should remove the incentives that have been built into our system to aid rapid exploitation of virgin materials; they have encouraged excessive use of materials in general and lent false economic advantages to virgin as opposed to recycled materials.

Removing these incentives will mean higher prices, but these should be carefully distinguished from inflationary increases. They reflect the embedding in prices of the social costs of particular goods and services, which now fall upon consumers.

20. See Clifford S. Russell and Walter O. Spofford, Jr., "A Quantitative Framework for Residuals Management Decisions," in Allen V. Kneese and Blair T. Bower (eds.), *Environmental Quality Analysis: Theory and Method in the Social Sciences* (Johns Hopkins Press for Resources for the Future, 1972). See also Allen V. Kneese, Robert U. Ayres, and Ralph C. d'Arge, *Economics and the Environment: A Materials Balance Approach* (Johns Hopkins Press for Resources for the Future, 1970).

The most important area for such reform is depletion allowances. Producers of most mineral products, such as lead, zinc, copper, and bauxite, can deduct from their gross incomes a substantial allowance for depletion, thereby reducing the effective tax rate they pay. This practice provides a major subsidy to the price of a number of resources, and thus encourages the excessive use of virgin materials as well as aH materials generally. It appears not only that depletion allowances are entirely inappropriate to our current circumstances but also that much can be said for federal efforts to strengthen the hands of the states in instituting or raising severance taxes.

To open a second front in the war on perverse incentives, we should directly and systematically encourage conservation of environmental media. A fully coherent set of effluent charges is not possible at the moment, but levying such charges on a broad front would recognize the interdependencies among the environmental media and promote processes that consume fewer materials or that are more conducive to recycling, as well as treatment of residual materials where appropriate.

A very promising start in this direction is contained in a bill recently introduced by Congressman John H. Heinz III of Pennsylvania. The bill would amend the Internal Revenue Code to levy "a tax on the discharge of taxable items . . . by any stationary or non-stationary source of pollution into the atmosphere or into or upon the navigable waters of the United States, adjoining shorelines, the contiguous zone, or the ocean."[21] The bill sets up a procedure for determining the tax rates to be set by Congress and calls for review at intervals. While it needs considerable elaboration, its direction is clearly right.

Eliminating subsidies for exploiting virgin materials and imposing across-the-board effluent charges could have a powerful effect on conservation of resources and improvement in environmental quality. Such actions would also have the desirable efficiency effects that we have previously discussed.

Present legislation tries to deal with all these problems, and to influence the whole vast array of decision makers involved, through direct regulation and subsidies. If this approach stands, it will, we believe, open a field day for lawyers, incur heavy costs, require a

21. H.R. 635, January 1973.

huge bureaucracy to give it any chance of success, impose ad hoc and capricious impacts, and involve far-reaching intrusion of the government into decisions about the design of industrial processes.

We do not suggest that an incentive-oriented approach could deal alone with all of the sticky problems that arise in achieving environmental control objectives. As we have pointed out, the discharge of highly toxic substances would still have to be prohibited by law and regulation. Schedules of effluent and emission charges that truly minimized the costs of pollution control would be too complex for practical application; the consequent simplified schedules would inevitably introduce some inefficiencies into the system. Because the current production techniques and locations of industrial firms are based on a world in which effluent and emission charges do not exist, the introduction of charges would probably have to be gradual to avoid excessive disruption. Some allowance for temporary relief might be needed for hardship cases, thus reintroducing regulatory-type decisions during an interim period.

The advantage of the incentive approach is not that it is free of administrative problems nor that it can fully duplicate a theoretical least-cost solution. But on both of these counts it is superior to the regulatory alternative.

A Positive Program

We conclude with a list of steps the federal government could take on the road to effective, efficient, and continuous management of our environmental resources. A few of these steps are partially embodied in current legislation.

1. Eliminate the artificial price advantage that virgin materials now enjoy vis-à-vis recycled materials. Doing so would also tend to damp excessive materials use. Consider reversing the relative exploitation of these materials by the systematic use of severance taxes.

2. Develop a list of possibly deleterious substances in effluents that is as complete as practical. Require all who discharge substantial amounts to sample their effluents and report them to a special data center operated by the Environmental Protection Agency or some other suitable agency.

3. Develop a list of substances whose discharge is forbidden because it has deleterious effects that clearly outweigh its cost-saving

benefits. Toxic persistent organics and heavy metals would be prime candidates. Those toxic substances whose use cannot be practicably forbidden should be taxed at a high rate on the input side to make throwing them away very costly.

4. On substances whose discharge is not absolutely forbidden, or whose use is not controlled by input taxes, levy national effluent or emission taxes at levels that provide a genuine incentive for control. Special provision could be made to assist firms that suffer particularly adverse effects that they can demonstrate. Where emission taxes cannot practically be collected, taxes should fall on inputs leading to discharge of deleterious substances. It must be recognized, however, that placing the tax on anything but the pollutant itself narrows the range of possible responses.

5. Increase the burden of proof on producers of new products or processes to identify and report any substances associated with them that might have adverse effects on health or on the ecological system.

6. Use the proceeds of the emission taxes and, if necessary, other appropriated federal funds to encourage the establishment of pollution management agencies that cover whole regions. These might be states, where appropriate, and they could be defined in terms of environmental media such as air, water, and land; but requirements should be laid down to assure that interdependencies among airborne, waterborne, and solid wastes are appropriately recognized, and that efficient regional programs of control can be pursued. Once regional agencies are duly established, the task of collecting emission taxes would be turned over to them, and the proceeds made available to them. They would be permitted to raise some or all of the emission taxes but not to reduce them below the national level.

7. Enact national legislation, such as that passed in Michigan, repealing the public-nuisance doctrine which effectively prohibits suits by individuals against general "public nuisances" like air and water pollution.[22] Thus, legal approaches would have the benefit of a second line of defense against the inevitable failures of management agencies.

22. Sax, *Defending the Environment*, pp. 247–52.

8. Improve understanding of the functioning of natural systems affected by residuals discharge through research, models of the environment, and monitoring. The activities of the Environmental Protection Agency and the National Oceanic and Atmospheric Administration should be greatly extended in these areas.

9. Strongly support the development of national indicators that accurately reflect real changes in the state of the environment and the quality of life.

Appendix: A New Water Quality Law for West Germany

In the fall of 1973, a new water quality law was to be presented to the Parliament of the Federal Republic of Germany. The following paragraphs present the highlights of a discussion of the proposed law issued by the German Interior Ministry in July 1973.

The document discussed the advantages of a charges system over the permit and enforcement system that had been in effect in West Germany since 1957. Of special importance was the tendency of the proposed system to minimize costs by concentrating reductions where costs are lowest and by encouraging the development and installation of low-discharge technologies in industry. The potential result was the rationalization of the price structure that, under the previous system, favored processes that make heavy use of common-property resources by failing to exact payment for them.

The continuing decline in water quality in the Federal Republic lends even more weight to the new scheme, for it can be highly effective as well as efficient. The scheme levies fees on dischargers in accordance with the damaging effect of their waste waters, and sets the fees so that they will provide a strong stimulus to reducing waste discharges to watercourses. The choice of technologies for reducing or eliminating waste water discharges is to be left to the discharger. In other words, the system is designed to be technologically neutral and to motivate research and development for improved processes generating fewer residual materials.

Payments are to be made by all public and private dischargers of waste water to surface waters and coastal waters without regard to the legality of the discharge, or to the size or quality of the watercourses to which discharges are made.

The institution of treatment or other processes for controlling waste water can reduce the payment; but as long as there is any discharge, no matter how small, some payment must be made. Two reasons underlie this requirement: One is to maintain an incentive to the development of low-discharge technologies. The second is that otherwise the system, besides being inefficient, would be regarded as unfair to small dischargers; the residual waste material from a large enterprise might be larger than the total discharge from a small enterprise, and yet the larger and more destructive discharge would incur no penalty.

The level of the charge is to be uniform throughout the Federal Republic in an effort to make broad progress on reducing water pollution. Background material presented in the early part of the draft indicates that despite the existence of a permit and enforcement technique in the Federal Republic, discharges of waste water have continued to climb significantly. Also, uniform charges discourage industries from migrating from dirtier to cleaner areas, where the charges would otherwise be lower.

For an interim period of four years, the charge will be 25 German marks per population equivalent. This level of charge is regarded as just sufficient to spur construction of treatment plants at larger sources, although the stimulus to process change might be considerable even at smaller sources. Following this interim period, the level will rise to 40 marks per population equivalent, which would strongly stimulate the construction of full biological treatment plants for even small, or otherwise high-cost, discharge points.

The charge is suspended for a period keyed to the average time needed to construct a treatment plant. If the plant is constructed by that time, the charge will apply only to the remaining discharge. If it is not, the charge is to apply retroactively to the entire discharge.

The charges are to be based on reports by the dischargers themselves on their own discharges, supplemented by random checks. The proceeds will go to the Länder for improving water quality or diminishing the damages of waste discharges. The Bund and the Länder themselves will be charged for any discharges from facilities they operate.

The draft law also contains an appendix in which the formula for determining population equivalent is given. It resembles closely the formulas now used by the Genossenschaften to levy charges on waste dischargers in the Ruhr region. It weighs suspended material of both mineral and organic type with amounts of both biochemical and chemical oxygen demand. The appendix in the draft law does not include any toxic materials or pH in the formula. However, formulas discussed in earlier documents do include such factors. It is possible that the formula has not been settled at this point.[23]

23. A fairly full discussion of the Genossenschaft formulas is found in Kneese and Bower, *Managing Water Quality*.

Epilogue

THIS STUDY has dealt with the difficulties that have faced the nation and the Congress in designing effective and efficient programs to control environmental pollution. In the most general sense, the difficulties have arisen from the failure of legislation to take account of the great complexity of the environmental problem—the widely varying costs and techniques of pollution control, the numerous interactions among pollutants, and the subtle economic factors at work. We have identified four specific characteristics of current policy on pollution control that tend to reduce its effectiveness and efficiency.

First, there has been an almost exclusive reliance on detailed central regulation and on court enforcement as the principal techniques for limiting the discharge of pollutants. We have questioned the ability of a regulatory bureaucracy to cope effectively or efficiently with the complex and pervasive interactions between economic activity and the environment.

Second, policy on water pollution control has also emphasized generous federal subsidies for the construction of waste treatment plants by municipalities and industry. Neglect of policies to encourage efficient plant operations and failure to integrate the construction subsidies into region-wide plans for water pollution control have reduced the payoff from this federal investment.

Third, because most of the costs of pollution control do not appear in the federal budget, legislative deliberations about the targets for environmental quality and the techniques of control pay too little attention to costs. As a result we will end by paying too much for the environmental improvement we get and probably will get much less than the targets we have set.

Fourth, concentration on reaching ambitious goals very quickly has often taken precedence over long-run achievements, as in the case of auto emission controls. Freezing pollution control technology to meet tight deadlines, before adequately investigating all the alternatives, not only raises costs but puts at risk long-term environmental objectives.

These kinds of problems are not unique to environmental control policy. Increasingly, the American people are calling upon the federal government to accept at least some responsibility for a number of other aspects of social and economic performance that until quite recently were the concern solely of state and local governments or private industry. The supply and distribution of energy, railroad freight cars, health care, urban transportation, and manpower training are a few examples. To some extent increased governmental intervention in these and other areas arises from the urgent need to deal with the unwanted side-effects of economic growth and urbanization. It also stems from the adoption of more humane and ambitious goals for social performance. Whatever the cause, many of the problems that we have identified are not unique to the area of pollution policy.

Urban mass transportation is aided by federal subsidies for construction and equipment, which bias local decisions in the direction of excessively capital-intensive and costly mass transit systems. Shortages of railroad freight cars are dealt with by regulatory orders, seeking to direct empty cars from one part of the country to another. Health insurance programs are designed with little emphasis on incentives for efficiency, and centralized regulation grows geometrically in an attempt to cope with rising costs and fees.

The Sources of the Failure

Our examination of the development of pollution control legislation suggests several specific reasons why the federal government, especially the Congress, finds it difficult to design successful methods to intervene in complex social and economic relationships.

The Changing Nature of the Congressional Task

The first is that Congress's perception of its mission has not changed to meet the needs of an ever more complex society. In earlier periods the central task of lawmakers was to reconcile divergent views about what the federal government ought to do and how much it should spend. Should a social security program for the aged and the unemployed be initiated? Who should be covered?

How should it be financed? Should an interstate highway program
be started? How large should it be? Compromise, negotiation, and
bargaining about these matters were at the heart of the legislative
process. Because it was not mainly in the business of delivering
public services at the local level nor of influencing the details of
private industrial performance, the federal government could carry
out its domestic responsibilities in a fairly straightforward way,
usually by a centralized and hierarchical bureaucracy. Once the
outline of a social security system was hammered out, the choice of
administrative apparatus for keeping the appropriate records and
making benefit payments was not a major problem. Once a highway program was agreed to, the technical problems could be left to
the engineers. Lawmakers rightly concentrated upon the basically
political problems of securing agreement among groups with widely
different views about what the federal government ought to do. How
the government should go about accomplishing the agreed-on task
was not usually a critical issue, because the job itself was not technically difficult.

More recent forms of social intervention have thrust new burdens
upon lawmakers. Air and water pollution is an extremely complex
phenomenon. How successfully and how efficiently pollution is reduced will depend not just on the kind of goals set or on a few key
decisions by Washington civil servants but upon tens of thousands
of individual actions taken by business firms and municipalities
throughout the country. Reform of the health delivery system, and
successful operation of any federal health insurance program, cannot be made to hinge upon some centralized and relatively simple
control apparatus—the system is far too complicated. Devising a
national energy policy requires not only good judgment about
broad goals but also great technological and economic knowledge.
Securing consensus on *what* the federal government ought to do is
no longer a sufficient criterion for successful legislation. Deciding
how the job should be done has become an equally difficult and
critical issue. The design of effective and efficient policy instruments
can no longer be expected to flow solely from the good intentions or
the simple common sense of individual lawmakers who are negotiating with each other.

The Congress itself does not have the facilities, by way of staff
or technical assistance, to develop or to evaluate alternative ap-

proaches to the increasingly complex questions of economic and social policy. The staffs of congressional committees are chosen principally for their talent in helping to devise and negotiate legislation that secures a consensus broad enough to assure passage. While this kind of talent is an immensely valuable asset and adequate to policy problems whose technical aspects are not crucial, it does not afford the Congress the help it needs on more intricate issues. Nor are the other sources of technical assistance now available to Congress effectively used to fill this gap. Technical assistance from agencies of the executive branch is often valuable, but it is unlikely to provide an objective evaluation of alternatives and options at odds with those proposed by the administration. The Congress is, in part, at the mercy of the executive branch in this regard. Similarly, congressional hearings are essentially structured to meet the needs of a time when the major legislative task was to find ways of reconciling the divergent views of various interests and pressure groups. This is still an important function, but it is not enough. The hearings process, with its adversary and question-and-answer flavor, is not a fruitful means by which comprehensive alternatives can be designed and evaluated.

Several consequences flow from the lack of independent technical and analytic assistance available to the Congress. First, the range of alternatives that the Congress examines is often very narrow. While novel proposals are often put forward by individual members of the House or Senate, congressional committees naturally feel reluctant, when the chips are down, to spend much time examining innovative policy techniques, since they have no independent capability of developing or evaluating them. Second, the Congress lacks the capability of estimating the economic costs of various proposals, especially when they are not budgetary costs. Since economic costs are seldom known, much less considered, the political advantage goes to the sponsor of the most ambitious targets. Third, in committee or in conference, the hectic process of negotiating the last-minute compromises needed for winning a majority often ends in hastily conceived and drafted legislative provisions. When the Congress is dealing with difficult social or economic problems, the absence of staff resources to subject these last-minute changes to technical analysis can lead to particularly ineffective or inefficient legislative programs.

Congress and the Marketplace

A second reason for the failure to devise effective instruments of social intervention lies, we believe, in the reluctance of the Congress to use markets and the price system as instruments of public policy. The need for social intervention often arises because private markets are not working well—or because, as chapter 1 pointed out, they work with marvelous efficiency, but in the wrong direction. But rather than correct the price system—by levying effluent charges, for example—and thereby redirect incentives toward socially desirable ends, the Congress is most likely to reach for the old tried (if not true) remedies. In the case of environmental control this tendency led to emphasis on regulation and construction subsidies. And when this approach did not appear to be working well the response was simply to intensify it by increasing the power of the regulators and enlarging the grants, rather than by undertaking a basic reexamination of its efficacy.

One reason for the congressional propensity to rely upon regulation as the solution to complex social problems is the fact that most congressmen are lawyers. In recent years from 55 to 60 percent of the members of the Senate and the House have had a legal background. Superficially, it seems perfectly reasonable that lawmakers should be drawn principally from the ranks of lawyers. Yet the legal approach to certain types of social problems can sometimes be highly inappropriate. In some ways the legal and the economic approaches to questions stand in sharp contrast to each other. Legal training necessarily, and quite properly, concentrates on the specification of rights and duties in law or in regulations, and on the case-by-case adjudication of individual situations in the light of the law and the regulations. If it is in society's interest to change social behavior, lawyers go about the task by changing the specified rights and duties. The economic approach stresses not rights and duties but incentives. People or firms act in certain ways because their self-interest dictates doing so. In this light, changes in social behavior can be accomplished by modifying the incentives that induce people to act. Usually the legal and economic approaches are complementary; each has its proper sphere as a means of governing social activity. But sometimes they are competitive—they represent alternative ways of achieving the same objective. The fact that the incentive approach is often given such short shrift in favor of the regulatory approach is hardly unexpected in view of the predominance of lawyers in the Congress.

What Can Be Done?

No simple structural set of changes in the Congress could itself produce more workable solutions to the kinds of problems we have discussed here. We have no panaceas. There is, however, a major prerequisite for an improvement in the legislative process. Congress needs to become aware of the two basic "facts of life" that we have stressed in this study. First, problems such as environmental control or health care involve extremely complicated economic and social relationships. Policies that may appear straightforward—for example, requiring everyone to reduce pollution by the technologically feasible amount—will often have ramifications or side-effects that are quite different from those intended. Second, given the complexity of these relationships, relying on a central regulatory bureaucracy to carry out social policy simply will not work: there are too many actors, too much technical knowledge, too many different circumstances to be grasped by a regulatory agency. While some framework of regulations will usually be needed, effective legislative solutions will also have to concentrate on devising incentives under which individuals and business firms, in their own self-interest, make socially desirable decisions.

To avoid misunderstanding we hasten to point out that the issue at stake here is not the strength or weakness of federal pollution control policy. The fact that federal regulation has proven an ineffective control instrument does not imply that the regulatory powers now in federal hands should be turned over to fifty state governments. Paradoxically, the day-to-day decisions about pollution abatement can be left to individuals and business firms only after strong federal action has given them fundamentally new incentives and institutions to which they can respond.

Beyond a general change in attitudes toward the way in which social issues can be handled, certain alterations in the way Congress operates could improve the effectiveness of social intervention in such areas as environmental control.

The first of these is so simple, and so often urged, that it sounds banal. The technical qualifications of the staffs available to congressional committees should be radically improved. Proposals have been made to assign responsibility for program evaluation and technical analyses to the General Accounting Office or the Legislative Reference Service of the Library of Congress. Technical assistance functions can be performed by these institutions, but only if there exist technically capable staffs who report directly to the relevant committees and who know what kind of research help is needed and what is available. While the task of some congressional staff members must remain what it is now—assisting in negotiation —many more staff members should be analytically oriented. They must be capable of developing and evaluating alternative approaches to program design, and of bringing together estimates of program costs and consequences. With competent analytic staffs at their disposal, congressional committees could also begin to use fruitfully the huge resources of the executive branch. At the present time, the analyses and estimates presented to the Congress by executive agencies must always be slightly suspect. Necessarily they reflect some combination of administration positions and bureaucratic interests. But staff members who can formulate the right questions, spot critical assumptions, and ferret out embarrassing weak points can afford to rely on the executive agencies for much of the needed spadework, since they would be—or could become —expert enough to monitor the quality of the results.[1] Moreover, analytically oriented staff could draw upon the work done at universities and private research institutions.

While the indirect and more remote economic consequences of fundamental social changes like environmental control cannot be foreseen, many of the more important impacts can be at least roughly estimated. Various kinds of large-scale economic models have been used to gauge the effect of alternative policies for air and water pollution control on the prices, costs, and investment requirements of particular industries, and on individual communities, river basins, and airsheds. Unfortunately, in most cases these relatively complicated analyses have been done at research institutions, universities, or government agencies *after* rather than *before* enact-

---

1. The analytic and technical assistance provided the House Ways and Means and Senate Finance Committees by the staff of the Joint Committee on Internal Revenue Taxation is a case in point.

ment of the policies they were designed to analyze. Seldom have such studies been available to congressional committees as a legislative tool, helping them to assess the advantages and disadvantages of alternative policy proposals. Under normal circumstances the development and application of these large-scale models could not be undertaken by congressional staffs themselves. But a competent staff would know what the possibilities are and could arrange for their development by outside private or governmental institutions. Equally if not more important, such a staff could interpret the findings of these studies and apply them to the relevant legislative issues. All too often, large-scale technical studies that could have been valuable in legislative development have simply gathered dust in some forgotten filing cabinet because no one was available to make the link between the technical findings and the political realities of the congressional committee room.

While the last paragraphs have emphasized the importance of providing Congress with realistic estimates of the costs and economic consequences of its actions, we do not mean to slight the need for better assessment of the social problems that call for federal intervention. The analytic help that competent staffs can lend the legislative process need not be conservatively biased, stressing costs and ignoring potential benefits. The essential point is that the newer tasks of the federal government are inherently so complex that successful legislative action to deal with them requires a larger component of technical and analytic sophistication than was typically the case in the past. The role of technical know-how and analysis is to supplement, not to replace, political savvy and social conscience.

Conclusions

It is not surprising that a society of increasing population, interdependence, and affluence should discover the need for collective intervention in matters once ignored or left wholly to private decisions. Pollution, congestion, noise, sprawling suburbs, and the decay of central cities are not the dominant problems of a young and sparsely settled nation. And concentration on economic growth was likely to be balanced by considerations of environmental quality, the provision of decent housing for the poor, and other more recent concerns only after the growth itself had generated the re-sources to address these problems.

While the nation's attention has turned to the need for new types of social policy, we have generally proceeded as if the legislative process and the techniques for governmental action suitable for an earlier set of problems could be carried over without change. But cleaning up the environment, relieving urban congestion, and re-forming the health care system are not the same kinds of tasks as building canals and highways and paying out social security benefits. And the legislative genius that finds ways to mold a coalition behind a piece of legislation, though still necessary, is no longer sufficient to devise the instruments of social intervention.

Throughout this study we have used the issue of environmental control to illustrate the failures of the traditional legislative ap-proach to policy formulation and to suggest the kinds of changes that are needed. Our recommendations for reform can be briefly summarized. First, Congress can no longer get by on political skills alone. It must supplement those skills with staff resources competent to provide the technical and analytic help that is absolutely essential in dealing with difficult social issues. Second, the blunt instrument of central regulatory controls is not an effective legisla-tive device to accomplish federal intervention in complex economic relationships. Far more than in the past, legislative action must em-phasize the creation of new incentives and new institutions that harness the self-interest of individuals and business firms toward socially desirable goals.

Index

Aeration, 25, 29, 87

Agriculture, pollution from feedlot run-off, 16, 25, 75, 87

Air pollution: by automobiles, 3, 16, 46–48, 64–66; cost of controlling, 70, 73–75; difficulty in tracing, 11–12, 17–18; emission-charge approach to, 98–105; enforcement of regulations for, 49–50, 51–53; legislation for, 45–50, 51–53; meteorological conditions and, 17; mobile versus stationary sources for, 25–26. *See also* Ambient standards; Automobile emissions; Emission standards

Air Pollution Control Act (*1955*), 46

Air Quality Act (*1967*), 48–50, 98

Algae, 15

Ambient standards, 17; for air, 49, 51; explanation of, 18; for water, 39

Aspin, Les, 100

Automobile emissions, 3, 16; cost of controlling, 73–74, 80; government action to control, 45–46, 47–48, 52–53; industry action to control, 46, 48, 64; problems in enforcing regulations on, 64–65; problems in maintaining pollution control devices for, 101; smog tax on, 101–03; suggested methods for controlling, 25–26; travel restrictions to reduce, 68, 75

Automobile Manufacturers Association, 46, 48

Ayres, Robert U., 105n

Basic oxygen furnace, residuals from, 24

Basin-wide firm, 85–87

BAT. *See* Best-available-technology standard

Beet sugar industry: cost of reducing BOD discharges, 19–20, 23; recycling to reduce BOD discharges, 24

Best-available-technology (BAT) standard: cost of, 70n; difficulty in establishing, 63; guidelines for, 60; need for continuous improvements in, 82–83; *1983* requirement for, 61

Best-practicable-technology (BPT) standard: cost of, 72–73; guidelines for, 60; *1977* requirement for, 61

Biochemical oxygen demand (BOD): cost of reducing, 19–20, 23, 71, 81–82, 88–89; explanation of, 13–14; factors influencing amount discharged, 14–15; industrial generation of, 42, 43; models to determine safe amounts of, 17; recycling to reduce, 24; removal of, 42

BOD. *See* Biochemical oxygen demand

Bower, Blair T., 44n, 81n, 89n, 98n, 107n, 111n

BPT. *See* Best-practicable-technology standard

Cadmium poisoning, 15

California, air pollution, 46–47

Capehart, Homer E., 46

Carbon monoxide, 16, 52, 65

Carlson, Jack W., 99n

Cement plants, emission standards for, 59

Clean Air Act (*1963*), 47

Clean Air Amendments (*1970*), 1, 46, 50, 100; provisions of, 51–52

Coal: pollutants from mining, 75; sulfur-oxide emissions from burning, 16, 26

Common-property resources: explanation of, 4; price system as incentive for overuse of, 5–6; scarcity of, 5, 11

Conference on the Potomac, 40

Congress: lack of technical assistance for, 114–15; reliance on regulation

121

Pollution, Prices, and Public Policy

Paper mills, water pollution from, 5–6
Particulates, 16–17
Penalties, for pollution violations, 53, 54, 64
Pesticides, 16
Petroleum refinery, cost of reducing BOD discharge from, 20, 23
"Pindex" method of weighting pollutant toxicity, 104
Plant nutrients, as pollutants, 15, 43
Polikoff, Alexander, 41n
Pollutants: categories of, 13–16; difficulty in tracing, 11–12, 17–18; global effects of, 12–13; monitoring of, 13; persistent, 16; "pindex" method of weighting toxicity of, 104; threshold value of, 51; sources of, 17–18. *See also* Air pollution; Residuals; Wastes; Water pollution
Pollution. *See* Air pollution; Water pollution
Pollution control: comprehensive policy for, 105–07; criteria for, 12; differing views on, 9–10; distribution of benefits from, 27–28; economic aspects of, 19; objectives of, 11; proposed federal programs for, 107–09; reconciling economic growth with, 3, 9; regional agencies for, 2, 6, 44, 96–97; relaxation of standards for, 75–76; shortcomings of current policy for, 112–13; techniques for, 23–26; use of mathematical models in, 17–18, 118–19. *See also* Cost of pollution control; Effluent charges; Emission charges; Legislation; Subsidies
Potomac River Basin study, 87
President's Commission on National Goals, 2
Prices: effect on common-property resources, 5–6; effect of pollution control on, 28, 71
Proxmire, William, 97, 100
Public Works Subcommittee on Air and Water Pollution, Senate, 47
Pure Air Tax Act of *1972,* 99

Quarles, John R., Jr., 59, 63n

Rand Corporation, 101
Rauch, Robert J., 61n, 62
Recycling, 24, 37, 105, 106
Refuse Act (*1899*), 30; enforcement of, 39–40

Regional management: advantages of, 86–87, 104; for air quality, 2, 49; for land-use planning, 6, 44; for water quality, 2, 6, 44–45, 90, 96–97
Regulatory approach to pollution control, 1; criteria for, 12; shortcomings of, 7, 93, 112. *See also* Enforcement of antipollution regulations; Legislation
Renshaw, Edward F., 93n
Research, on pollution control, 46, 54
Residuals: degradable, 13–15; explanation of, 4; management program for, 105; nondegradable, 15; persistent, 16. *See also* Wastes
Reuss, Henry S., 39
Rice, cadmium poisoning from, 15
Rivers. *See* Watercourses
Ruckelshaus, William, 64
Russell, Clifford S., 20n, 24n, 105n

San Francisco Bay study, 87
Sax, Joseph L., 97n, 108n
Schmookler, Jacob, 24n
Schneider, A. M., 104n
Shapley, Deborah, 66n
Shellfish, 33, 41
Smelters, emission standards for, 59, 67
Spofford, Walter O., Jr., 105n
State governments: cost of waste treatment plants, 72; federal pressure on, to improve environment, 45; implementation plans to meet antipollution standards, 52; plans for urban transportation restrictions, 67–68; priorities for allocation of water quality subsidies, 35–36; problems in enforcing antipollution regulations, 66–67
Steel manufacturing, generation of residuals by, 24
Steinbrunner, John, 53n, 65n 103n
Subsidies, water treatment plant construction, 1, 8, 34; amount of, 42; authorization for, under Water Pollution Control Act Amendments of *1972,* 54–55; importance of enforcement action to accompany, 35, 37; shortcomings of, 35–38, 112
Sulfur-oxide emissions, 16, 17, 26, 59, 67; cost of reducing, 82; taxation of, 99–100

Taxation: of automobile smog, 101–04; to cover cost of pollution control, 71, 76; of damaging discharges, 2,

Pollution, Prices, and Public Policy

ALLEN V. KNEESE
and CHARLES L. SCHULTZE

Over the past fifteen years the federal government has developed policies to reduce air and water pollution that rely heavily on very detailed regulation of polluters and on generous subsidies for the construction of waste treatment plants. In this study Allen V. Kneese and Charles L. Schultze argue that the combination of regulations and subsidies is an expensive and ineffective way to deal with air and water pollution.

After summarizing the economic and technical background necessary to understand the pollution control problem, the authors review the legislative history of federal pollution control efforts and discuss the high costs and enforcement difficulties that plague those efforts. They propose alternative policies designed to change economic incentives and institutions so that individuals, business firms, and municipalities would find it in their own interest to reduce pollution. The proposed incentives take the form of effluent and emission charges—stiff taxes levied on each unit of pollutant discharged into the air or water. The authors also propose the establishment of federally sponsored regional authorities charged with developing overall plans for air and water pollution control. Finally, viewing air and water pollution as examples of a much broader class of complex social problems, they examine why Congress has trouble designing legislative solutions and suggest some means of improving congressional performance.

Allen V. Kneese, professor of economics at the University of New Mexico, was until May 1974 director of the Quality of the Environment program at Resources for the Future, Inc. Charles L. Schultze is a senior fellow in the Brookings Economic Studies program and a professor of economics at the University of Maryland. The book is a joint project of Resources for the Future and the Brookings Institution.

THE BROOKINGS INSTITUTION
WASHINGTON, D.C.

ISBN 0-8157-4993-7